RELIGIOUS FOLK-SONGS OF THE NEGRO

AMS PRESS
NEW YORK

RELIGIOUS FOLK-SONGS OF THE NEGRO

AS SUNG AT HAMPTON INSTITUTE

EDITED BY

R. NATHANIEL DETT, Mus. D.

HAMPTON INSTITUTE

HAMPTON INSTITUTE PRESS
HAMPTON, VA.
1927

Library of Congress Cataloging in Publication Data

Dett, Robert Nathaniel, 1882-1943, ed.
  Religious folk-songs of the Negro as sung at
Hampton Institute.

  Reprint of the 1927 ed.
  1. Negro songs. I. Hampton Institute, Hampton,
Va. II. Title.
M1670.H3 1972   784.7'56   72-1595
ISBN 0-404-09920-3

Reprinted from the edition of 1927, Hampton
First AMS edition published in 1972
Manufactured in the United States of America

International Standard Book Number: 0-404-09920-3

AMS PRESS INC.
NEW YORK, N. Y.   10003

DEDICATION

To the Negro Youth of America

and especially of

HAMPTON INSTITUTE

*whose aspiration has been for me
one of the chief sources of inspiration,
this book is affectionately dedicated,
with the hope that the mantle of faith
thrown down from the ofttimes weary
but never broken spirit of our forefathers
may continue to shield and clothe
those of generations yet to come.*

CABIN AND PLANTATION SONGS AS SUNG BY THE HAMPTON STUDENTS

PREFACE TO FIRST EDITION (1874)

The slave music of the South presents a field for research and study very extensive and rich, and one which has been scarcely more than entered upon.

There are evidently, I think, two legitimate methods of treating this music: either to render it in its absolute, rude simplicity, or to develop it without destroying its original characteristics, the only proper field for such development being in harmony.

Practical experience shows the necessity, in some cases, of making compensation for its loss in being transplanted. Half of its effectiveness in its home depends upon accompaniments which can be carried away only in memory. The inspiration of numbers; the overpowering chorus, covering defects; the swaying of the body; the rhythmical stamping of the feet; and all the wild enthusiasm of the Negro camp-meetings,—these evidently cannot be transported to the boards of public performance. To secure variety and do justice to the music I have therefore treated it by both methods. The most characteristic of the songs are left entirely or nearly untouched. On the other hand the improvement which a careful bringing out of the various parts has effected in such pieces as "Some o' Dese Mornin's," "Bright Sparkles in de Churchyard," "Dust and Ashes," and "The Church of God," which seemed especially susceptible to such development, suggests possibilities of making more than has yet been made out of this slave music.

Another obstacle to its rendering is the fact that tones are frequently employed which we have no musical characters to represent. Such, for example, is that which I have indicated as nearly as possible by the flat seventh in "Great Camp-Meetin'," "Hard Trials," and others. These tones are variable in pitch, ranging through an entire interval on different occasions, according to the inspiration of the singer. They are rarely discordant and often add a charm to the performance. It is of course impossible to explain them in words, and to those who wish to sing them the best advice is that most useful in learning to pronounce a foreign language, *Study all the rules you please, then—go listen to a native.*

One reason for publishing this slave music is that it is rapidly passing away. It may be that this people which has developed such a wonderful musical sense in its degradation will in its maturity produce a composer who can bring a music of the future out of the music of the past. At present, however, the freedmen have an unfortunate inclination to despise it as a vestige of slavery; those who learned it in the old time, when it was the natural outpouring of their sorrows and longings, are dying off; and if efforts are not made for its preservation the country will soon have lost this wonderful music of bondage.

The melodies in this book, with a few exceptions, are published here for the first time, and the exceptions are themselves original in arrangement and effect. The words of the slave hymns are often common property through the South, but are sung to different tunes in different sections of the country.

THOMAS P. FENNER

HAMPTON, VA., January 1, 1874

CABIN AND PLANTATION SONGS AS SUNG BY THE HAMPTON STUDENTS

PREFACE TO EDITION OF 1891

In publishing this new and enlarged edition of the Hampton Songs, little explanation is needed, for it is done in response to a demand. Ever since the publication of the first edition in 1874, when the band of Hampton Student Singers was helping to raise the walls of Virginia Hall by its concerts in the North, there have been frequent requests for this music. Meanwhile, though the old favorites have not been neglected, many more melodies, striking and beautiful, have been brought in by students from various parts of the South. The field seems almost inexhaustible. Their origin no one exactly knows. An old "aunty," questioned on the subject, declared that "when Mass'r Jesus walked de earth, when He feel tired He sit a-restin' on Jacob's well and make up dese yer spirituals for His people." A half-familiar strain, recalling some old ballad or psalm-tune, now and then suggests a possible solution for some of them; and, as Lowell said of Chaucer, "If one can transmute lead into gold, why ask where he got his lead?" So strikingly original, as well as of such quaint, pathetic, even artistic beauty, are most of them, that they justify Edward Everett Hale's assertion that they are "the only American music."

Some of the most beautiful of those now sung at Hampton, for the music of which we are frequently asked, are now published for the first time. They have been arranged by Mr. F. G. Rathbun, of Hampton, for the last six years instructor of the school choir and band.

To these are added, also, a number of the Tuskegee Students' songs, arranged by Mr. R. H. Hamilton, a graduate of Hampton Institute, one of its first band of student singers and for several years leader of its choir, now occupying the same position at the Tuskegee Normal School, Alabama. Some account of that institution, founded by Hampton graduates, will be found in the introduction to its songs, on another page.

A consideration of the slave music of the South, from the musician's standpoint, was made by Mr. Thomas P. Fenner, who trained the original band of Hampton Student Singers and arranged the songs in the first edition of this book, his preface to which is reprinted here. After the fifteen years that have passed since he wrote, the

[vii]

disposition which he noticed in the freedmen to be ashamed of the songs of slave times still exists. Some of the old ring is lost with the experience that called it forth. Yet the people are still natural musicians, and it is easy to arouse in the more advanced an intelligent interest in the characteristic music which excites so much sympathy and respect for their race, and which is so identified with their past history and their present fortunes.

The Hampton School has more than one field of interest for the musician as well as the ethnologist. The two or three Indian songs which Mr. Rathbun has reduced to notation, are interesting specimens of these wild chants evanescent and untamable as the wind in the pines.

A few other songs of nationalities represented in Hampton's "Girdle Around the World" are thought to be of sufficient interest to be introduced.

HELEN W. LUDLOW

HAMPTON INSTITUTE, VA., Jan. 1, 1891

RELIGIOUS FOLK-SONGS OF THE NEGRO AS SUNG BY THE HAMPTON STUDENTS

PREFACE TO EDITION OF 1909

For the fifth time we are publishing these "Religious Folk-Songs of the Negro." To this edition are being added some twenty-five new ones, for the use of which we wish to acknowledge the courtesy of Professor F. J. Work of Fisk University, Mrs. Jennie C. Lee of Tuskegee Institute, the Calhoun Colored School, Ala., and the Penn School, S. C.

It is exceedingly gratifying to know that these songs and Negro folklore generally are not only continuing to hold their own among white people but are becoming more and more popular with Negroes. General Armstrong often referred to the plantation songs as a wonderful possession which the Negro should hold on to as a priceless legacy. They are truly a priceless legacy. Though the words are sometimes rude and the strains often wild, yet they are the outpourings of an ignorant and poverty-stricken people whose religious longings and ideals struggled for expression and found it through limited vocabularies and primitive harmonies. They are not merely poetry, they are life itself—the life of the human soul manifesting itself in rude words, wild strains, and curious though beautiful harmonies.

For nearly a score of years I have led the plantation songs at Hampton Institute and, while in a general way we adhere to the music as notated in this book, we find that the best results are usually obtained by allowing the students, after they have once caught the air, to sing as seems to them most easy and natural.

ROBERT R. MOTON

Commandant

HAMPTON INSTITUTE
Hampton, Va., May 11, 1909

RELIGIOUS FOLK-SONGS OF THE NEGRO AS SUNG AT HAMPTON INSTITUTE

FOREWORD

I

The Negro folk-songs in this volume are arranged in a sequence whose order differs, I believe, from that of any previous publication. The regarding of the songs as actual hymns makes such an arrangement not only possible, but natural, even inevitable, and it was this underlying conception of them and the fact that they are so used at Hampton Institute, which was the inspiration of the idea in the mind of the editor.

The captions of the various groups are such as might be found in any church hymnal and while it is true that the songs of themselves offer much that is novel in the way of poetry, melody, harmony, and rhythm, fundamentally it will be discovered that they correspond in sentiment with all the basic ideas of orthodox religious dogma.

According to Romain Rolland,* "The political life of a nation is only the most superficial aspect of its being. In order to know its interior life it is necessary to penetrate to its soul through literature, philosophy, and the arts, for in these are reflected the ideas, the passions, and the dreams of a whole people."

Were it not for this tendency on the part of historians to omit or ignore the influence of religion on the events which their annals are intended to record, such a classification as the one presented here might have appeared long ago; for it must be conceded to be a mistake not to include in any system of tabulations of human affairs, the action of those psychological forces which through the ages have swayed various peoples one way or another. "The earliest records of primitive man," says the late Honorable Henry Bingham, LL. D., "present him as a religious being. Impressed with awe at the wonders of the heavens above him and the earth around him, the inner intelligence breathed into man at his creation made him realize the presence of an unseen hand that controlled all things."

That the Negro, rudely transplanted from African to American shores had such a realization, even a casual perusal of these songs will show; but his ability unwaveringly to believe in and love and praise "the unseen hand that controlled all things" when it seemed

* Romain Rolland, "Musiciens d'Autrefois."—Translation by Edward Dickinson

most evident that that hand was especially turned against him, also reveals, even to those entitled to insight by racial inheritance, a religious faith almost past understanding.

It is a well-known fact that humanity is most prayerful in the hour of need. Religion comes then as the reverberation of a great cry of soul; which explains in brief the Negro spiritual, which more than almost any other folk-music in the world is a great cry of soul whose burden is of age-old promises of eternal freedom, of feasts of milk and honey, and of the divine glory of a love all-inclusive.

"Folk-songs," says the late Henry E. Krehbiel," are the echoes of the heart-beats of the vast folk and in them are preserved feelings, beliefs, and habits of vast antiquity, not only in the words, but also in the music and perhaps more truthfully in the music than in the words. Music cannot lie, for the reason that the things which are at its base, the things without which it could not be, are unconscious, unvolitional human products." Folk-songs, then, quite aside from their music value, are of inestimable worth because of the light which they throw upon those individualizing elements in the character of the race that produced them.

II

But as such an index of character, Negro music, at the very outset, made a bad start. The singing and dancing in a New Orleans theatre of "Jim Crow," a Negro folk nonsense-ballad by a Negro cripple who was able to flop himself about the stage in imitation of the motions of a crow, was such an uproarious success that it was imitated throughout the country by "black-face" comedians of both races as a sure-fire hit. Thereby an early tradition of the Negro as essentially a humorous character was established, the effect of which exists to the present day.

Romanticists who have pictured the bondsman as a happy, carefree being have seen in the ecstatic expression of his song an extension of this established idea and so have added their bit in emphasizing the supposedly rollicking nature of his contribution.

An old book of minstrel songs reveals the fact that almost all of them are meant to be Negro in character, but they are hilarious and insincere. The melodies are interrupted only that the singer may "do the buck." The most unfortunate feature is that many are out-and-out parodies of Negro church songs. The words of one run:—

> "Monkey dressed in soldier clothes
> All cross over Jordan
> Went in de woods to drill some crows
> O Jerusalem——"

another begins with:—

> "Angels meet me at the crossroads
> Don't charge sinner any toll——"

and is followed by sixteen measures of an instrumental jig. In still another, there is a graphic account of Gabriel's blowing his horn "early in de mornin' " and all of the sinners are warned to be present to

> "Jine in de army fo' dey close de door
> Ob de big white house on de todder shore."

Between the verses of this, there is also an instrumental polka of eight measures.

The fact that one minstrel company* alone, featuring such songs as those above quoted, ran eight consecutive years in New York, that the ditties of Stephen Foster have enjoyed world-wide popularity, that some of the Broadway shows run by Negroes themselves have dance-parodied their own religious music for commercial appeal, reveals something of what has been, and to a large extent still is, the popular idea of the Negro and his music.

But in the delineation of character, if truth rather than mere effect for effect's sake, is the end desired, too much emphasis must not be laid upon any one element which may later be found to be but a mere phase. Human nature, even in primitive peoples, is more or less complex and cannot be revealed by a sort of peep-show exhibition which permits but one part to be seen at a time, any more than a picture of a countenance can be impressed on the intelligence of an onlooker by the single revelation of one feature at a time, such as an ear or an eye. The stage character of the Irishman and the Jew, which graced (or disgraced) the American stage a decade or so ago never existed in real life; neither did, or does, the Negro character as embodied in the familiar and conventional stage "darkey." But as thousands of people have no other source of information except the theatre or popular fiction (which employs a similar method) these pseudo-types finally come to be accepted as true.

So the average audience almost everywhere expects the Negro to be funny. All things associated with him, and all things which he has made, being supposedly created in a mind but dimly lit with the half-light of a feeble intelligence or stimulated by emotions which were, or are, but the reflections of the emotions of others around him, are presumed consequently to be taken humorously, even as the words of a child who accidentally hits upon a great truth are expected to be taken.

In those primitive Negro churches where original songs are still sung, there is often hand-clapping, patting and rattling of the feet, swaying of the body, and sometimes, but rarely now, snapping of the fingers in accompaniment. The attention of visitors or casual

* Rice's Minstrels

observers is generally attracted by these obvious and dramatic evidences of emotion, and they are amused by them because it is the style to be amused, and because Americans have rather formed the bad habit of laughing at other people or at almost anything which is "different"; but being too far removed from the actual spirit of the song by this very lack of sympathy (in the broader sense of the word) they entirely miss the real essence of what is going on.

Such visitors are like those who, standing on a hill-top, watch a bonfire in the valley below; they enjoy all the visual effects of the conflagration but feel none of its heat.

It was once the privilege of the writer to attend a backwoods "after-service" at which, when the regular service had "let out," a small group of not more than seven or ten (they were all old women if he remembers rightly) grouped themselves together by standing in a ring with a criss-cross clasping of hands. To the strong rhythm of a sort of chant, they violently thrust each other backwards and forwards with an intense fervor. There was no shuffling of feet or rotating of the ring as described by Mr. Johnson,* but the effect was crudely fantastic, savoring of a barbaric incantation. But this I soon forgot, for, looking into the faces of the singers, I was struck by evidences of spiritual elevation, and I realized that in some mysterious way these unlettered people, by a common consent, were mutually enjoying a communion with eternal forces by a method of evocation beyond the reach of the uninitiated.

III

That the Negro as a race had, and still has, an outlook on life which is quite his own, and that his songs express moods born of his own peculiar experience and which are quite original with him, may strike many as new. But how, otherwise, shall one explain the strong, unwavering note of hope of final recompense, and the assurance of the perfectness of another life to come, unless one is willing to admit that the slave brought with him from Africa a religious inheritance which, far from being shaken in any way, was strengthened by his American experience? Does it seem natural to suppose that there could be anything in slave life, not only as it existed in our Southern States, but even in slave life as it has existed anywhere in the world, to inspire such an idea? It was nothing else, then, than this religious inheritance, this oriental regard for parable and prophecy, which made easy the incorporation into the spiritual of so much of Bible story; for in striving to give voice to his experiences the slave found in the Testaments, in the story of the children of Israel, for instance, much in the way of a text that was ready made; all of which was quite to his liking though, of course, unconsciously, for he could thus sing of one thing and mean another. This indirect mode of

* James Weldon Johnson, "The Book of American Negro Spirituals"—Preface

[xiii]

expression, it is well known, is one of the most characteristic earmarks by which the art of the East is distinguished from that of the West; it is characteristic of Negro music, often hiding, mask-like, its fundamental mood and not a little of its real meaning.

There are many songs, however, in which the Negro's soul-sorrow is hidden by no mask. How poignantly it is revealed in "Farewell, farewell to my only child"; how prayerfully in "O Lord, O my Lord, keep me from sinking down"; how filled with longing in "Deep River! My home is over Jordan, Lord, I want to cross over into camp ground"; with what philosophical self-analysis in "Sometimes I feel like a motherless child" or in "I'm troubled in mind; if Jesus don't help me, I surely will die."

IV

What this ability of the black man to improvise his troubles into art-forms has fully meant to him will probably never be told. Very likely it served as a sort of safety valve for his pent feelings, saving the country from an even greater tragedy than that precipitated by the Civil War, and himself from a disaster equally great.

"O glorious solace of immense distress
A conscience and a God,"

cries Dr. Watts, and his words are profoundly true. But the worth of native Negro genius to America is paramount; for certainly it is most important that in a country given over to commercial enterprise, there should be at least one wellspring of spiritual issue.

To the world is brought a great message of goodwill, for one of the most outstanding characteristics of all the songs is that, free as the music is from cacophony and discord, just as remarkably free is its poetry from any word of bitterness, anger, or reproach.

It seems that the glory of the Christian religion in the framework of the Negro spiritual is as the effect of the stained-glass window in the wall of the sanctuary. As forms of cosmic interest are thus excluded and the interior made more beautiful by a mellow and suggestive neutral tint, even so does the Negro folk conception of the doctrines of Christ, though often crudely expressed, exclude all forms of hatred, vengeance, rebellion, or dislike, mollifying the high lights of the Old Testament, along with those of life itself, into one composite hue whose tone is at once rich and colorful, warm and sof'

So the Negro, as revealed in his songs, continues to hold an enlarging interest, and in this there is nothing of an unnatural order, since he, in making a song to fit his own needs, has inadvertently voiced the cry of the world.

V

It is now generally conceded that this music is original to the Negro, in so far as any folk-music is original. Of those who sometimes still assert that the Negro folk idioms are derivations of revival hymns the question might pertinently be asked: Where is that wonderful matrix of hymnology out of which has grown these song jewels of Negro spirituals? It has long been accepted as scientifically true that the black man brought his musical idiom with him from his native land as he must have brought his susceptibility to religious suggestion. It would, of course, be unreasonable to suppose that this idiom was entirely unaffected by environment. But if it received, it also gave. In "Slave Songs of the United States" we read: "The words of the fine hymn 'Praise Member' (a Negro melody) are found with very little variation in 'Choral Hymns' (a standard hymnbook of the late sixties)." The editor of this collection informs us, however, that "*many of his songs were learned from Negroes in Philadelphia*," and Lt.-Colonel Trowbridge tells us that he "*heard this hymn before the war among colored people in Brooklyn.*"

In an old Baptist hymnal in Kentucky the editor once saw the words of "Not all the blood of beasts," set to a pentatonic tune which had all the characteristics of a Negro melody; and in a Methodist hymnal, recently in use in Tennessee, besides the familiar setting known to all, "How firm a foundation" appears to an alternative tune traditional with colored people.

William Francis Allen, one of the first to compile a collection of Negro folk-tunes, as early as 1867 writes, "The greater number of songs which have come into our possession seem to be the natural and original production of a race of remarkable musical capacity—imbued with the mode and spirit of European music, often nevertheless retaining a distinct tinge of their native Africa. The words are from Scripture and from hymns heard at church, expressions we find abundantly in Methodist hymnbooks, but with much searching I have been able to find hardly any trace of the tunes." Subsequent investigation by such authorities as H. E. Krehbiel, Henry T. Burleigh, Natalie Curtis (Burlin), Ballanta Taylor, James Weldon Johnson, and others confirm this conclusion as to the original quality of Negro music.

VI

The arrangements in this book are for unaccompanied choruses because practically all Negro folk-singing is unaccompanied group singing. A word on the manner of conducting, therefore, does not seem out of place.

For the most part, Negro music consists of a series of pulses, all of which are alike. That is, the secondary beats are as strong as the primary, or perhaps it would be still better to say that there are no secondary beats. The rhythm of the songs might very well be compared to that of the human pulse which is a series of throbs all of equal intensity.

When a song is once set in motion, its rhythm becomes immutable, the pause, especially in the refrain in which all join, being almost unknown. The singing sometimes begins a fraction slower than its regular tempo, but not markedly so. Sometimes there is, however, a feeling that a song is gaining in momentum until a certain rate is reached which is then maintained until the end.

Feeling for tempo is an inheritance with Negroes, as it is with most people, and if this natural feeling has not been disturbed by outside influences, it may be trusted to a large extent by the leader. It becomes the conductor's chief duty, then, merely to set the chorus in motion, and by easy and natural beats, which need be only occasional, keep them going and up to time.

Expressive singing, especially of solo lines, should be encouraged, as this is one of the means of achieving much of interest and variety in a form of music which, regardless of race, is universally characterized by monotony. Besides, it is an established tradition in the folk-music of all peoples that the effect of any song depends largely on the way it is sung, but anything like mimicry or characterization should not for a moment be tolerated; the members of the chorus should be led to appreciate the idea that folk-music is essentially *soul music* which they, having made their own, are to help others enjoy and understand.

Dr. Robert R. Moton, principal of Tuskegee Institute, who for many years as the "Major" was the leader of the "plantation singing" at Hampton Institute, was in many ways ideal in this capacity, as he has since proved himself to be in many others. He sang many of the solo lines in a voice which, though uncultivated, was powerful and expressive. Often, after getting the chorus of a thousand voices going, he would place both hands behind his back, leaving the singers to carry on in their own way, and the resultant freedom and informality seemed never to fail in adding a certain zest to the singing. His beat was inconspicuous.

One must deplore much of the present-day singing of these songs on the concert platform. So few of the artists of either race seem willing to trust alone to the inherent beauty of the music to make its own appeal; still fewer seem to realize that music which has come from the heart of one people, will go by its own strength to the heart of another; that such music needs no mannerisms or stage tricks to help it on its way.

VII

It has often been said that no one else can sing Negro songs as Negroes sing them, and the reason given is that Negroes being peculiar in physical make-up are supposed to emit a certain different kind of sound from all other species of the human animal, thus giving their song a unique quality impossible of duplication.

The writer has had over twenty years' experience of coming in daily contact for several hours at a time with Negro voices. He has taught fair Negroes who sang low and dark Negroes who sang high; Negroes with fine features who had coarse, almost unmanageable voices, and Negroes, aboriginal in appearance, possessed of fine, expressive voices. He has kept no tabulation of the relation of voices to noses and mouths but is convinced that there is nothing in the theory of physical appearance. Caruso with full, rounded features represents the tenor in opera while Amato with a face like a cameo stands for the baritone. Roland Hayes and John McCormack do not look alike and yet their voices are very similar. If physiognomy cannot be trusted as a guide to individual musical differences, how can it be as a true indicator or racial or group variation? Yet there does seem to be a difference in the singing by members of various races, which seems especially noticeable in group-singing. The Negro choir has a certain rich quality, as has also the Russian choir, when compared with choruses of other peoples.

This, the writer is convinced, is due more to a certain innate psychological capacity to react to the suggestion of the text than to anything else. Oppressed peoples are usually sympathetic, so are those from warm climates, and this sympathy shows in the voice. In another way it may be observed even by the unmusical: Many a person hearing a friend sing a new song can tell almost immediately by the sound of the voice whether or not the song has been well learned; the fact that the singer is not in thorough accord with the message he is trying to deliver making such a difference in voice quality as to be observed even by the merest tyro.

VIII

One of the most encouraging signs of our times is the apparent awakening of the mind of the public in regard to the true meaning of Negro folk-songs. The idea that the Negro spiritual has a message worthy of serious attention seems to be becoming more and more widespread. A recent protest of the press, both Negro and white, against the incorporation of these songs into some of the popular Broadway musical revues, is indicative of an increasing regard for their religious significance which made the spirituals appear strikingly out of place in the artificial and flippant atmosphere of the extravaganza.

It may be that the religious music of the Negro will add a new note to ecclesiasticism, as the secular music of the Negro has done to the affairs of everyday life. From the time of the plantation days to the present, the world has been cheered by the individual note of jocularity which has made unique the ragtime of America's minstrelsy and street songs and the jazz of her dance-halls and music comedies.

Even so, from the religious music of the Negro, from the aptly named "spirituals," may come as equally welcome a heart-quickening note to give new life to hymnology.

That it was an error, centuries ago, on the part of the church to divorce religious music from rhythmic utterance, no one will now deny; even so, the most popular hymns ever have been those with a more or less pronounced rhythm. The Negro spiritual, combining as it does religious feeling with a regular, almost irresistible beat, based on a scale in existence five hundred years before Christ, having its own simple harmonies and archaic cadences, presents in an elemental form the solution of one of the great problems of Christianity; how to evolve a style of music that will convey a religious message through a popular medium without at the same time suggesting things of the world.

In such a volume as this there is an opportunity, not only of experiencing the original psalms of suffering as born in the Negro breast, but also a greater opportunity of touching, as it were, the fringes of the robes of Grandeur, whose garments trail the dust but whose face, uplifted above the clouds, we are not yet permitted to see.

IX

The harmonizations and tunes in this book are as they are sung at Hampton Institute where the singing of these songs has been traditional since 1868. If there are slight differences, here and there, from other publishers' versions it is because every locality is a law unto itself on these points.

Some hitherto unpublished melodies, from the editor's own collection, appear for the first time. As these were written down from solo singing and as the singer did not know the other parts they are reproduced unharmonized.

It would seem that it might have been quite simple to have taught these songs by rote and let the students harmonize them by instinct; but one must remember that the young Negro student of today is not quite the slave of yesterday; a different outlook on life, the influence of the white man's education, of the concert-hall, the phonograph, and the radio, all in conjunction with the adventurous spirit characteristic of all youth, makes one hesitate to accept present-day arrangements as authentic, even though done by natives. Furthermore it has already been pointed out that it was a religious "urge" born of a great experience which gave rise to these songs; not having this experience it is impossible to get, and unreasonable to expect, a duplication of the primary effect.

This also explains why much of the present-day singing by colored people lacks something of the depth, sincerity, and pathos which marked that of other days and of which lack, many, remembering, justly complain. It is hoped that the publication of these melodies in their natural and untarnished settings will do much to revive and preserve this important element.

R. NATHANIEL DETT

HAMPTON INSTITUTE, March 14, 1926

INDEX OF SUBJECTS

NOTE 1 — Hymns on pages 118, 140, 192, and 219 should be credited to the Calhoun Collection.

NOTE 2 — Hymns on pages 12 and 231 should be credited to the Fisk Collection.

INDEX OF TITLES

[xxi]

INDEX OF FIRST LINES

[xxvi]

RELIGIOUS FOLK-SONGS
OF THE NEGRO

Hymns of Admonition

Babylon's Fallin'

'Pure cit-y, Bab-y-lon's fall-in', to rise no more,

'Pure cit-y, Bab-y-lon's fall-in', to rise no more.

Oh, Bab-y-lon's fall-in', fall-in', fall-in', Bab-y-lon's fall-in', to

Hymns of Admonition

De Ole Sheep Done Know de Road

Oh, de ole sheep done know de road, De

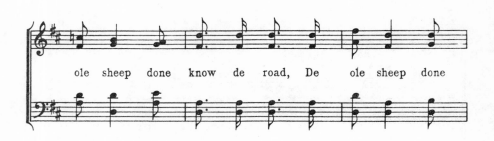

ole sheep done know de road, De ole sheep done

know de road, De young lambs mus' find de way.

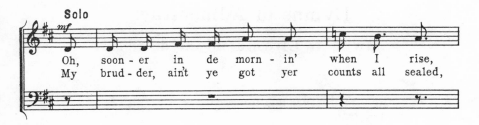

Oh, soon - er in de morn - in' when I rise,
My brud - der, ain't ye got yer counts all sealed,

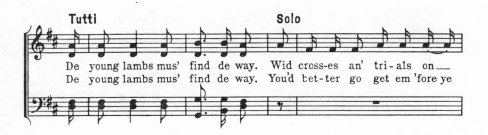

De young lambs mus' find de way. Wid cross-es an' tri - als on ___
De young lambs mus' find de way. You'd bet-ter go get em 'fore ye

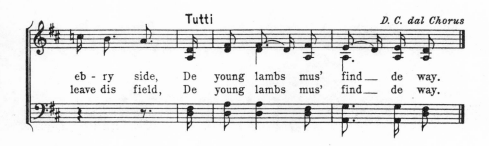

D. C. dal Chorus

eb - ry side, De young lambs mus' find ___ de way.
leave dis field, De young lambs mus' find ___ de way.

2

Oh, shout my sister, for you are free, De young lambs, etc.
For Christ hab bought your liberty, De young lambs, etc.
I raly do believe widout one doubt, De young lambs, etc.
Dat de Christian hab a mighty right to shout, De young lambs, etc.
      Chorus — Oh, de ole sheep, etc.

3

My brudder, better mind how you walk on de cross, De young lambs, etc.
For your foot might slip, an' yer soul git lost, De young lambs, etc.
Better mind dat sun, and see how she run, De young lambs, etc.
An' mind don't let her catch ye wid yer works undone, De young lambs, etc.
      Chorus — Oh, de ole sheep, etc.

Hymns of Admonition

Gwine to Live Humble to de Lord

Solo

mp semplice

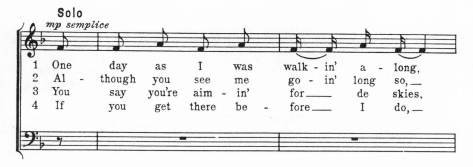

1 One day as I was walk-in' a - long,
2 Al - though you see me go - in' long so,
3 You say you're aim - in' for____ de skies,
4 If you get there be - fore____ I do, ____

Tutti

mf   *mp*   *   *più cresc.*

Gwine to live hum-ble to de Lord. De el - e-ments o-pened an' de
Gwine to live hum-ble to de Lord. I have my tri - als____
Gwine to live hum-ble to de Lord. Why don't you stop that
Gwine to live hum-ble to de Lord. Look out__ for me__ I'm__

Tutti

mf   *p*   *D. C.*

love came down, Gwine to live hum-ble to de Lord.
here be - low, Gwine to live hum-ble to de Lord.
tell - in' lies, Gwine to live hum-ble to de Lord.
com - in' too, Gwine to live hum-ble to de Lord.

*This pause is not always observed in the singing of this song at Hampton Institute.— Editor

Hymns of Admonition

If You Love God, Serve Him

Transcribed by
R. Nathaniel Dett

cresc.

Come, go to glo-ry with me

Hal-le - lu-jah, Love an' serve de Lord.

molto parlante
mp

Good morn-in', broth-er trav'-ler, Pray tell me where you're bound. I'm

D.C.

bound for Ca-naan's hap-py land, And de en - chant-ed ground.

2

Oh, when I was a sinner,
I like my way so well;
But when I come to find out,
I was on de road to hell.
Chorus — I fled to Jesus — Hallelujah! etc.
Oh, Jesus received me, Hallelujah, etc.

3

De Father, He looked on de Son and smiled,
De Son, He looked on me;
De Father, redeemed my soul from hell;
An' de Son, He set me free.
Chorus — I shouted Hallelujah! Hallelujah, etc.
I praised my Jesus, Hallelujah, etc.

4

Oh, when we all shall get dere,
Upon dat-a heavenly sho',
We'll walk about dem-a golden streets,
An' nebber part no mo'.
Chorus — No rebukin' in de churches — Hallelujah, etc.
Ebery day be Sunday — Hallelujah, etc.

Hymns of Admonition

Keep a-Inchin' Along

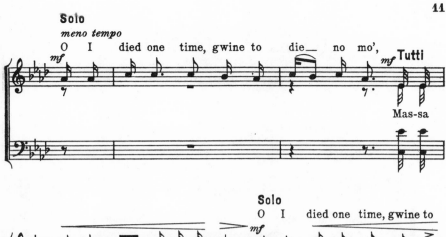

2

O you in de word an' de word in you,
Massa Jesus comin' by an' by;
O you in de word an' de word in you,
Massa Jesus comin' by an' by.
Chorus — Keep a-inchin', etc.

3

How can I die when I'm in de word?
Massa Jesus comin' by an' by;
How can I die when I'm in de word?
Massa Jesus comin' by an' by.
Chorus — Keep a-inchin', etc.

Hymns of Admonition

Live Humble

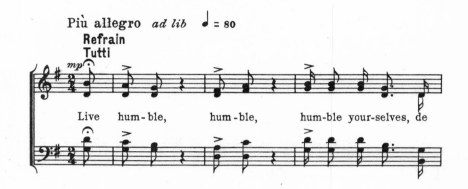

Live hum-ble, hum-ble, hum-ble your-selves, de

bell done ring, Live hum-ble, hum-ble, hum-ble your-selves, de bell done ring.

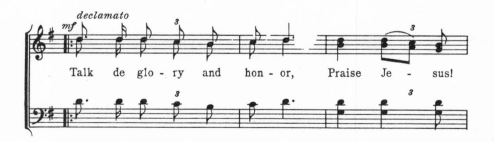

Talk de glo-ry and hon-or, Praise Je - sus!

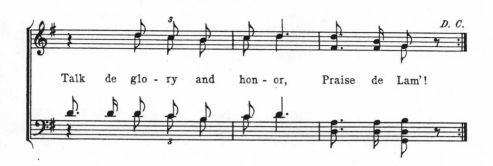

D. C.

Talk de glo - ry and hon - or, Praise de Lam'!

Solo
recitando rapido

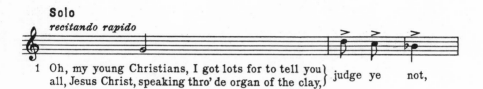

1 Oh, my young Christians, I got lots for to tell you all, Jesus Christ, speaking thro' de organ of the clay, } judge ye not,

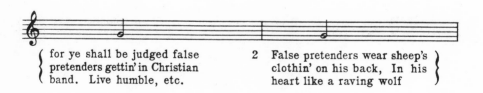

{ for ye shall be judged false pretenders gettin' in Christian band. Live humble, etc.

2 False pretenders wear sheep's clothin' on his back, In his heart like a raving wolf }

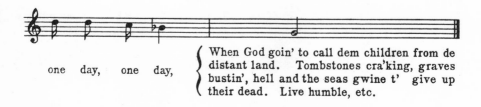

one day, one day,

{ When God goin' to call dem children from de distant land. Tombstones cra'king, graves bustin', hell and the seas gwine t' give up their dead. Live humble, etc.

Hymns of Admonition

Oh, de Downward Road Is Crowded

Moderato con moto ♩ = 88

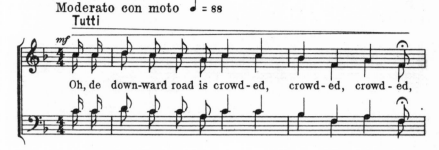

Oh, de down-ward road is crowd-ed, crowd-ed, crowd-ed,

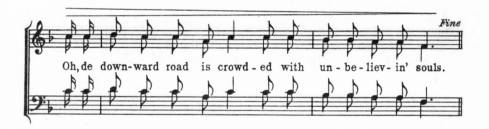

Oh, de down-ward road is crowd-ed with un-be-liev-in' souls.

Solo
meno tempo

1 Come, all ye way-ward trav'-lers, And let us jine an' sing,

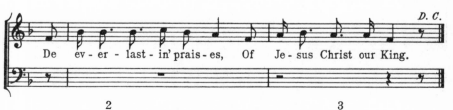

De ev-er-last-in' prais-es, Of Je-sus Christ our King.

2	3
Ole Satan's mighty busy,	When I was a sinner,
He follers me night and day,	I loved my distance well,
An' everywhere I pinted,	But when I come to fin' myself,
Dere's somethin' in my way.	I was hanging over hell.

Hymns of Admonition

Run to Jesus*

This song was given to the Jubilee Singers by Hon. Frederick Douglass, at Washington D.C., with the interesting statement that it first suggested to him the thought of escaping from slavery.

Run to Je - sus, shun the dan - ger, I

don't ex - pect to stay much long - er___ here.

1 He will be our dear-est friend, And will help us to the end, I

don't ex - pect to stay much long - er___ here.

2

Oh, I thought I heard them say,
There were lions in the way,
I don't expect, etc.

3

Many mansions there will be,
One for you and one for me,
I don't expect, etc.

*From the Fisk Collection, by permission

Hymns of Admonition

Oh, Sinner, You'd Better Get Ready

sin-ner must die; For it look-a like judg-ment eb-ry day.

mp Tutti — Solo *marcato*

Time is a-com-in' dat sin-ner must die; I heard a lumb'rin' in de sky,

Tutti — Solo

Time is a-com-in' dat sin-ner must die, Dat make-a me tink my

Tutti *mf* — *D. C. dal Segno*

time was nigh, Time is a-com-in' dat sin-ner must die.

2

I heard of my Jesus a many one say —
Time is a-comin' dat sinner must die,
Could 'move poor sinner's sins away —
Time is a-comin' dat sinner must die,
Yes, I'd rather a-pray myself away —
Time is a-comin' dat sinner must die,
Dan to lie in hell an' burn-a one day —
Time is a-comin' dat sinner must die.
Chorus — Oh, sinner, you'd better get ready, etc.

3

I think I heard-a my mother say —
Time is a-comin' dat sinner must die,
'Twas a pretty thing-a to serve de Lord —
Time is a-comin' dat sinner must die,
Oh, when I get to Heaven I'll be able for to tell —
Time is a-comin' dat sinner must die,
Oh, how I shun dat dismal hell —
Time is a-comin' dat sinner must die.
Chorus — Oh, sinner, you'd better get ready, etc.

Hymns of Admonition

Run, Mary, Run

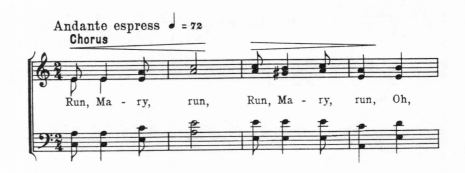

Run, Ma - ry, run, Run, Ma - ry, run, Oh,

run, Ma - ry, run, I know de od - er worl' 'm not like dis.

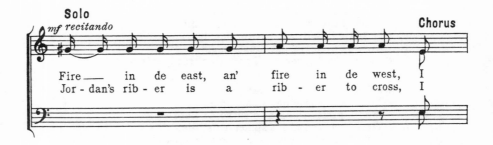

Fire —— in de east, an' fire in de west, I
Jor - dan's rib - er is a rib - er to cross, I

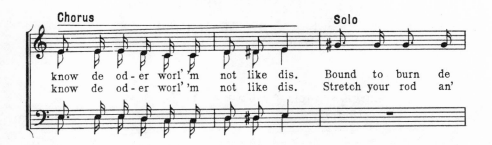

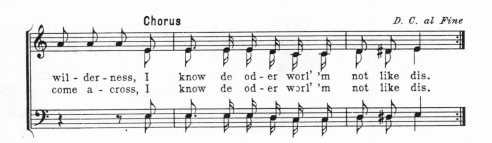

2

Swing low, chariot, into de east,
Let God's children hab some peace;
Swing low, chariot, into de west;
Let God's children hab some rest; } I know de oder worl' 'm not like dis.

3

Swing low, chariot, into de north;
Gib me de gold widout de dross;
Swing low, chariot, into de south;
Let God's children sing and shout; } I know de oder worl' 'm not like dis.

4

Ef dis day war judgment day,
Ebery sinner would want to pray;
Dat trouble it come like a gloomy cloud,
Gadder t'ick, an' t'under loud; } I know de oder worl' 'm not like dis.

Hymns of Admonition

Seek and Ye Shall Find*

Largo, sed tempo rubato ♩ = 44**

Refrain
Tutti

Seek, and ye shall find; Knock, and de door shall be o-pened;

Ask, and it shall be giv'n, And de Love come a-trick-al-ing down.

Basses octave lower last time

* From Tuskegee Collection, by permission
** The Tuskegee tempo mark was Andante. — Editor

2

‖: Elder, de Lord has been here, :‖
And de Love come a-trickaling down.
‖: Deacon, de Lord has been here, :‖
And de Love come a-trickaling down.
Seek, and ye shall find, etc.

3

‖: Preacher, de Lord has been here, :‖
And de Love come a-trickaling down.
‖: Class-leader, de Lord has been here, :‖
And de Love come a-trickaling down.
Seek, and ye shall find, etc.

Hymns of Admonition

Stay in de Field

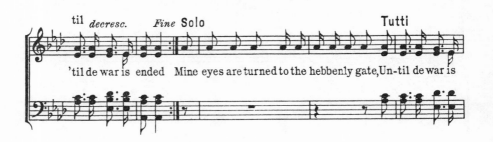

2

De tallest tree in Paradise, until de war is ended,
De Christian call de Tree of Life, until de war is ended.—*Refrain*

3

Green trees burning, why not de dry? until de war is ended,
My Saviour died, why not I? until de war is ended.—*Refrain*

Hymns of Admonition

Sun Don't Set in de Mornin'

Hymns of Admonition

Walk You in de Light

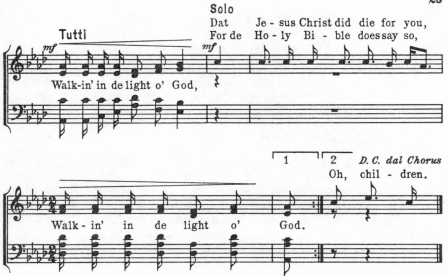

Solo
Dat Je - sus Christ did die for you,
For de Ho - ly Bi - ble does say so,

Tutti

Walk-in' in de light o' God,

Oh, chil - dren.

D. C. dal Chorus

Walk - in' in de light o' God.

2

I think I heard some children say,
    Walkin' in de light o' God,
Dat dey nebber heard de'r parents pray,
    Walkin' in de light o' God.
Oh, parents, dat is not de way,
    Walkin' in de light o' God,
But teach your children to watch an' pray,
    Walkin' in de light o' God.
Chorus — Oh, parents, walk you in de light,
        Walk you in de light, walk you in de light,
        Walkin' in de light o' God.

3

I love to shout, I love to sing,
    Walkin' in de light o' God,
I love to praise my Heavenly King,
    Walkin' in de light o' God.
Oh, sisters, can't you help me sing,
    Walkin' in de light o' God,
For Moses' sister did help him,
    Walkin' in de light o' God.
Chorus — Oh, sisters, walk you in de light, etc.

4

Oh, de heavenly lan' so bright an' fair,
    Walkin' in de light o' God,
A very few dat enter dere,
    Walkin' in de light o' God.
For good Elijah did declare,
    Walkin' in de light o' God,
Dat nothin' but de righteous shall go dere,
    Walkin' in de light o' God.
Chorus — Oh, Christians, walk you in de light, etc.

Hymns of Admonition

Walk Togedder, Childron

This hymn was made by a company of Slaves, who were not allowed to sing or pray anywhere the old master could hear them; and when he died their old mistress looked on them with pity, and granted them the privilege of singing and praying in the cabins at night. Then they sang this hymn, and shouted for joy, and gave God the honor and praise. — *J. B. Towe*

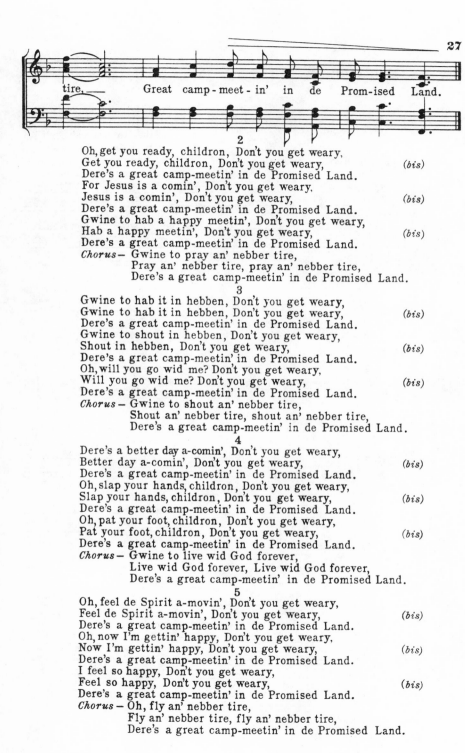

tire, ——— Great camp - meet - in' in de Prom-ised Land.

2
Oh, get you ready, children, Don't you get weary,
Get you ready, children, Don't you get weary,   *(bis)*
Dere's a great camp-meetin' in de Promised Land.
For Jesus is a comin', Don't you get weary,
Jesus is a comin', Don't you get weary,   *(bis)*
Dere's a great camp-meetin' in de Promised Land.
Gwine to hab a happy meetin', Don't you get weary,
Hab a happy meetin', Don't you get weary,   *(bis)*
Dere's a great camp-meetin' in de Promised Land.
Chorus — Gwine to pray an' nebber tire,
            Pray an' nebber tire, pray an' nebber tire,
            Dere's a great camp-meetin' in de Promised Land.

3
Gwine to hab it in hebben, Don't you get weary,
Gwine to hab it in hebben, Don't you get weary,   *(bis)*
Dere's a great camp-meetin' in de Promised Land.
Gwine to shout in hebben, Don't you get weary,
Shout in hebben, Don't you get weary,   *(bis)*
Dere's a great camp-meetin' in de Promised Land.
Oh, will you go wid me? Don't you get weary,
Will you go wid me? Don't you get weary,   *(bis)*
Dere's a great camp-meetin' in de Promised Land.
Chorus — Gwine to shout an' nebber tire,
            Shout an' nebber tire, shout an' nebber tire,
            Dere's a great camp-meetin' in de Promised Land.

4
Dere's a better day a-comin', Don't you get weary,
Better day a-comin', Don't you get weary,   *(bis)*
Dere's a great camp-meetin' in de Promised Land.
Oh, slap your hands, children, Don't you get weary,
Slap your hands, children, Don't you get weary,   *(bis)*
Dere's a great camp-meetin' in de Promised Land.
Oh, pat your foot, children, Don't you get weary,
Pat your foot, children, Don't you get weary,   *(bis)*
Dere's a great camp-meetin' in de Promised Land.
Chorus — Gwine to live wid God forever,
            Live wid God forever, Live wid God forever,
            Dere's a great camp-meetin' in de Promised Land.

5
Oh, feel de Spirit a-movin', Don't you get weary,
Feel de Spirit a-movin', Don't you get weary,   *(bis)*
Dere's a great camp-meetin' in de Promised Land.
Oh, now I'm gettin' happy, Don't you get weary,
Now I'm gettin' happy, Don't you get weary,   *(bis)*
Dere's a great camp-meetin' in de Promised Land.
I feel so happy, Don't you get weary,
Feel so happy, Don't you get weary,   *(bis)*
Dere's a great camp-meetin' in de Promised Land.
Chorus — Oh, fly an' nebber tire,
            Fly an' nebber tire, fly an' nebber tire,
            Dere's a great camp-meetin' in de Promised Land.

Hymns of Admonition
You Goin' to Reap Jus' What You Sow

Collected and transcribed by
the editor from the singing
of the Hampton students led
by Paige I. Lancaster

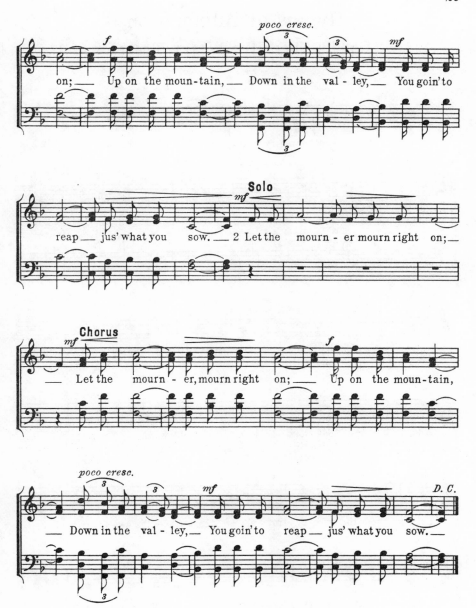

3 Let the deacon plead right on;

4 Let the preacher preach right on;

5 Let the liar lie right on;

Hymns of Admonition
Let Us Cheer the Weary Traveler

Let us cheer the wea-ry trav-el-er,___ Cheer the wea-ry trav-el-er;

Let us cheer the wea-ry trav-el-er, A - long the heav-en-ly way.

1 I'll take my gos - pel trum - pet, And I'll be - gin_ to blow,
2 And if you meet with cross - es And tri - als on_ the way,

And if my Sav-iour helps me, I'll blow wher-ev-er I go.___
Just keep your trust in Je - sus, And don't for - get_ to pray.

Let us cheer the wea-ry trav - el - er,___ Cheer the wea-ry trav-el - er;

Let us cheer the wea-ry trav-el-er, A - long the heav-en-ly way.

*At Hampton Institute the first two and a half measures are sung as a solo by the "leader"; the whole chorus joins in at the point marked. **

Hymns of Aspiration
Don't Leave Me, Lord

2
No use talkin' what you gwine t' do,
Don't 'tend t' 'ny my God for you.— *Refrain*

3
I don't wan' t' stumble an' I don't wan' t' stop,
I don't wan' t' be no stumblin' block.— *Refrain*

Hymns of Aspiration
Good Lord, Shall I Ever Be de One?

Moderato ♩=76
Tutti

Good Lord, shall I ev - er be de one? Good

Lord, shall I ev - er be de one? Good Lord, shall I

Fine

ev - er be de one, To get o - ver in de Prom - ise' Lan'?

Solo
mf

1 God placed A - dam in de gar - den, 'Twas a - bout de cool of de
2 The Lord walk - ed in de gar - den, 'Twas a - bout de cool of de

D.C

day, Call for ole A - dam, An' he tried to — run a - way
day, Call for ole A - dam, An' — A - dam said "Hear me Lord."

Hymns of Aspiration
I Want to Be Ready

Hymns of Aspiration
Gwine Up

Oh, saints an' sin-ners will-a you go, See de heb-ben-ly land,

I'm a gwine up to heav-en for to see my robe, See de heb-ben-ly land.

Gwine to see my robe an' try it on, See de heb-ben-ly land,

It's bright-er dan-a dat glit-ter-in' sun, See de heb-ben-ly land.

2
I'm a gwine to keep a-climbin' high—
  See de hebbenly land;
Till I meet dem-er angels in-a de sky—
  See de hebbenly lan'.
Dem pooty angels I shall see—
  See de hebbenly lan';
Why don't de debbil let-a me be—
  See de hebbenly lan'.
Refrain—Oh yes, I'm gwine up, etc.

3
I tell you what I like-a de best—
  See de hebbenly lan';
It is dem a-shoutin' Methodess—
  See de hebbenly lan';
We shout so loud de debbil look—
  See de hebbenly lan';
An' he gets away wid his cluvven foot—
  See de hebbenly lan'.
Refrain—Oh yes, I'm gwine up, etc.

Hymns of Aspiration
I Am Seekin' for a City

2

We will trabbel on together, Hallelujah,   *(bis)*
Gwine to war agin de debbel, Hallelujah,   *(bis)*
Gwine to pull down Satan's kingdom, Hallelujah, *(bis)*
Gwine to build up de walls o' Zion, Hallelujah. *(bis)*
Chorus.— Lord, I don't feel no-ways tired, etc.

3

Dere is a better day a-comin', Hallelujah,   *(bis)*
When I leave dis world o' sorrer, Hallelujah,   *(bis)*
For to jine de holy number, Hallelujah,   *(bis)*
Den we'll talk de trouble ober, Hallelujah.   *(bis)*
Chorus.— Lord, I don't feel no-ways tired, etc.

4

Gwine to walk about in Zion, Hallelujah,   *(bis)*
Gwine to talk-a wid de angels, Hallelujah,   *(bis)*
Gwine to tell God 'bout my crosses, Hallelujah, *(bis)*
Gwine to reign wid Him foreber, Hallelujah.   *(bis)*
Chorus.— Lord, I don't feel no-ways tired, etc.

Hymns of Aspiration

I Don't Want to Stay Here No Longer*

Andante ♩ = 66
Refrain
mf espress.

Oh, swing low, sweet cha - riot, Pray let me en-ter in, I don't want to stay here no long - er.

Fine

Solo

I done been to heav - en, an' I done been tried, I
Oh, down to de wa - ter I was led, my

been to de wa-ter, an' I been bap - tized,
soul got fed with de heav'n - ly bread,

---

* Also known as "The Danville Chariot" — **Editor**

D.C.

2

I had a little book, an' I read it through,
I got my Jesus as well as you;
　I don' want to stay here no longer;
Oh, I got a mother in de promised land,
I hope my mother will feed dem lambs;
　I don' want to stay here no longer.
　　Chorus — Oh, swing low, sweet chariot, etc.

3

Oh, some go to church for to holler an' shout,
Before six months dey're all turned out;
　I don' want to stay here no longer.
Oh, some go to church for to laugh an' talk,
But dey knows nothin' 'bout dat Christian walk;
　I don' want to stay here no longer.
　　Chorus — Oh, swing low, sweet chariot, etc.

4

Oh, shout, shout, de deb'l is about;
Oh, shut your do' an' keep him out;
　I don' want to stay here no longer.
For he is so much-a like-a snake-a in de grass,
Ef you don' mind he will get you at las',
　I don' want to stay here no longer.
　　Chorus — Oh, swing low, sweet chariot, etc.

Hymns of Aspiration
I Would Like to Read

Fine

I would like to read a sweet sto-ry of old.___

Solo *un poco declamato*   *più f*   **Tutti** *mf*   *cresc.*

1 Come on, brud-der, an' help me tell— Like to read a sweet

Solo *mf*

sto-ry of old, De sto-ry of-a King Man-u-el,___

Tutti *mp*   *D.C.*

I would like to read a sweet sto-ry of old.___

2
If ebber I get up on de other sho',
  Like to read a sweet story of old,
By de grace of God I'll come here no mo',
I would like to read a sweet story of old.
                    Refrain

3
I des wan' to get up on de mountain top,
  Like to read a sweet story of old,
I'll praise my God an' nebber stop,
I would like to read a sweet story of old.
                    Refrain

Hymns of Aspiration
In Bright Mansions Above

Moderato molto con pieta ♩ = 72

Refrain
Tutti
mp   poco cresc.

In bright man - sions a - bove, In bright man - sions a - bove,

Lord, I wan' t' live up yon - der, In bright man - sions a - bove.

Fine

Solo
più cresc.

1 My moth - er's gone to glo - ry, I wan' t' go there too,
2 My fa - ther's gone to glo - ry, I wan' t' go there too,
3 My sis - ter's gone to glo - ry, I wan' t' go there too,

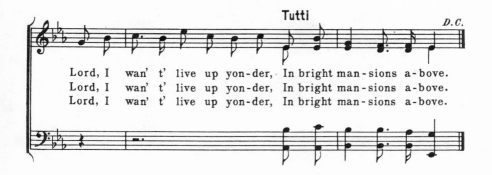

Lord, I wan' t' live up yon-der, In bright man-sions a-bove.
Lord, I wan' t' live up yon-der, In bright man-sions a-bove.
Lord, I wan' t' live up yon-der, In bright man-sions a-bove.

4

My brother's gone to glory,

I wan' t' go there too, Lord,

I wan' t' live up yonder,

In bright mansions above.

5

My Saviour's gone to glory,

I wan' t' go there too, Lord,

I wan' t' live up yonder,

In bright mansions above.

N.B. After the *D.C.* the Refrain generally begins thus

In-a bright man-sions etc.

Hymns of Aspiration
Let de Heaven Light Shine on Me

Largo con voglia ♩=54

Let de heav-en light shine on me,___ Let de

heav-en light shine on me, For low is de way to de

up-per bright world, Let de heav-en light shine on me.

1 Oh,_ brud-der, you must bow so low,___
2 Oh,_ sis-ter, you must bow so low,___
3 Oh,_ preach-er, you must bow so low,___

Brud-der, you must bow so low, For low is de way to de
Sis-ter, you must bow so low, For low is de way to de
Preach-er, you must bow so low, For low is de way to de

up-per bright world, Let de heav-en light shine on me.
up-per bright world, Let de heav-en light shine on me.
up-per bright world, Let de heav-en light shine on me.

4
Class leader, you must bow so low,
Class leader, you must bow so low,
For low is de way to de upper bright world,
Let de heaven light shine on me.
Chorus—Let de heaven light shine on me, etc.

5
Oh, elder, you must bow so low,
Elder, you must bow so low,
For low is de way to de upper bright world,
Let de heaven light shine on me.
Chorus—Let de heaven light shine on me, etc.

6
Oh, deacon, you must bow so low,
Deacon, you must bow so low,
For low is de way to de upper bright world,
Let de heaven light shine on me.
Chorus—Let de heaven light shine on me, etc.

Hymns of Aspiration
Look Away

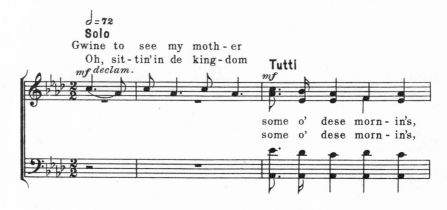

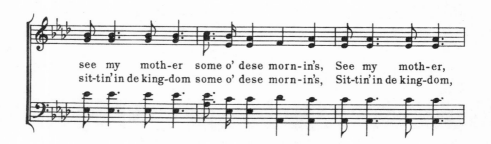

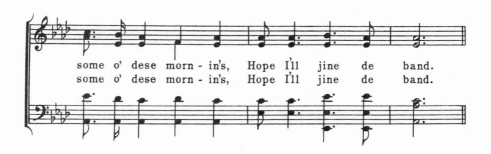

2
Gwine to see my brother some o' dese mornin's,
Oh, shouting in de heaven some o' dese mornin's,

3
Gwine to walk about in Zion some o' dese mornin's,
Gwine to talk-a with de angels some o' dese mornin's,

4
Gwine to talk de trouble ober some o' dese mornin's,
Gwine to see my Jesus some o' dese mornin's,

Hymns of Aspiration

Reign, Massa Jesus

O reign, O reign, O reign, my Sav-iour, Reign, Mas-sa Je-sus, reign,

O reign sal-va-tion in my soul, Reign, Mas-sa Je-sus, reign.

1 I nev-er shall for-get that day, Reign, Mas-sa Je-sus, reign.
2 I look'd at my hands and my hands look'd new, Reign, Mas-sa Je-sus, reign.
3 I nev-er felt such love be-fore, Reign, Mas-sa Je-sus, reign.

When Je-sus washed my— sins a-way, Reign, Mas-sa Je-sus, reign.
I look'd at my feet and they look'd so too, Reign, Mas-sa Je-sus, reign.
Say-ing, "Go in peace and sin no more, Reign, Mas-sa Je-sus, reign.

Hymns of Aspiration
Lord, I Want to Be a Christian

Andante espressivo, molto quasi preghiera ♩=68-76

Solo					
1 Lord,	I	want	to	be	a
2 Lord,	I	want	to	be	more
3 Lord,	I	want	to	be	more
4 I	don't	want	to	be	like
5 Lord,	I	want	to	be	like

Chris-tian
lov - ing
ho - ly
Ju - das
Je - sus

In - a	my	heart,	in - a	my	heart, Lord,	I
In - a	my	heart,	in - a	my	heart, Lord,	I
In - a	my	heart,	in - a	my	heart, Lord,	I
In - a	my	heart,	in - a	my	heart, I	don't
In - a	my	heart,	in - a	my	heart, Lord,	I

want to be a Chris-tian In-a my heart.____
want to be more lov-ing In-a my heart.____
want to be more ho-ly In-a my heart.____
want to be like Ju-das In-a my heart.____
want to be like Je-sus In-a my heart.____

Refrain

In-a my heart, _____ In-a my heart, _____

In-a my heart, In-a my heart.

Lord, I want to be a Chris-tian In-a my heart.____
Lord, I want to be more lov-ing In-a my heart.____
Lord, I want to be more ho-ly In-a my heart.____
I don't want to be like Ju-das In-a my heart.____
Lord, I want to be like Je-sus In-a my heart.____

Hymns of Aspiration

Roll, Jordan, Roll*

Collected and transcribed by
the editor from the singing
of the Hampton students led
by Paige I. Lancaster

2
O sister, you ought t'have been there,
Yes, my Lord!
A-sitting in the kingdom
To hear ole (when) Jordan roll.
Refrain

3
O preacher, you ought t'have been there,
Yes, my Lord!
A-sitting in the kingdom
To hear ole (when) Jordan roll.
Refrain

4
O sinners, you ought t'have been there,
Yes, my Lord!
A-sitting in the kingdom
To hear ole (when) Jordan roll.
Refrain

* See Appendix for the scoring of the original version of this song. This version, while possibly less striking, is by far the more popular. — Editor

** It is not infrequent or unusual on the repeats for the chorus to join in the melody with the solo (leader). — Editor

Hymns of Aspiration

Want to Go to Heaven When I Die

Transcribed by the editor from
the singing of the Hampton students
led by Paige I. Lancaster

Ben ritmo ♩ = 72

1 Want to go to heav-en_ when I die, Want to go to heav-en
2 Want to see my moth-er_ when I die, Want to see my moth-er
3 Want to see my fa-ther when I die, Want to see my fa-ther
4 Want to see my sis-ter when I die, Want to see my sis-ter
5 Want to see my Je-sus when I die, Want to see my Je-sus

when I die, Want to go to heav-en_ when I die; Good Lord,
when I die, Want to see my moth-er_ when I die; Good Lord,
when I die, Want to see my fa-ther when I die; Good Lord, when I
when I die, Want to see my sis-ter when I die; Good Lord,
when I die, Want to see my Je-sus when I die; Good Lord,

Refrain
molto fervore

die. Good Lord, when I die, Good Lord, when I die, Good

Solo
Shout it o-ver **Tutti**

1.   2. *Fine*

Lord, when I die, Good Lord, when I die! Good die!

Hymns on Biblical Themes

Daniel Saw the Stone

Poco allegro con anima ♩ = 88

Refrain
Tutti

Dan-iel saw the stone, Roll-ing, roll-ing,

Dan-iel saw the stone, Cut out the moun-tain with-out hands. *Fine*

Solo *parlante semplice* — **Tutti**

1 Nev-er saw such a man be-fore, Cut out the moun-tain with-out hands,
2 Dan-iel pray'd in the li-ons'den, Cut out the moun-tain with-out hands,
3 Dan-iel pray'd three times a day, Cut out the moun-tain with-out hands,

Solo *simile* — **Tutti** — *D. C.*

Preach-ing gos-pel to the poor, Cut out the moun-tain with-out hands.
Spite of all those wick-ed men, Cut out the moun-tain with-out hands.
Drive the dev-il far a-way, Cut out the moun-tain with-out hands.

Hymns on Biblical Themes

Down by the River

3

Pilate called for water to wash his hands,
 Down by the river;
"I find no fault of this good man,"
 Down by the river side.
Refrain —

4

O fishin' Peter led the way,
 Down by the river;
But nothing was caught till the break of day,
 Down by the river side.
Refrain —

5

Sister Mary wept and Martha cried,
 Down by the river;
When Christ the Lord was crucified,
 Down by the river side.
Refrain —

6

When we meet in the middle of the air,
 Down by the river;
We hope to meet our friends all there,
 Down by the river side.
Refrain —

Hymns on Biblical Themes

Band ob Gideon

The explanation which has been given us of the origin of this curious hymn is, we think, invaluable as an example of the manner in which external facts grew to have a strange symbolical meaning in the imaginative mind of the Negro race.

In a little town in one of the Southern States, a Scriptural panorama was exhibited in which Gideon's Band held a prominent place, the leader being conspicuously mounted upon a white horse. The black people of the neighborhood crowded to see it, and suddenly, and to themselves inexplicably, this swinging "Milk-White Horses" sprang up among them, establishing itself soon as a standard church and chimney-corner hymn. — *Thomas P. Fenner*

2
Duo —   I hail to my brudder, my brudder he bow low,
          Saying, don't you want to go to hebben? —
          How I long to see dat day!
Chorus — Oh, ride up in de chariot, ride up in de chariot,
          Ride up in de chariot ober in Jordan;
          Ride up in de chariot, ride up in de chariot —
          How I long to see dat day!
          It's a golden chariot, a golden chariot,
          Golden chariot ober in Jordan;
          Golden chariot, a golden chariot —
          How I *long* to see dat day!

3
Duo —   I hail to de mourner, de mourner he bow low,
          Saying, don't you want to go to hebben? —
          How I long to see dat day!
Chorus — Oh, de milk an' honey, milk an' honey,
          Milk an' honey ober in Jordan;
          Milk an' honey, milk an' honey —
          How I long to see dat day!
          Oh, de healin' water, de healin' water,
          Healin' water ober in Jordan;
          Healin' water, de healin' water —
          How I *long* to see dat day!

Hymns on Biblical Themes

De Ole Ark a-Moverin' Along

Moderato ♩ = 72
Solo
parlante sed con giusto

Jes' wait a lit-tle while, I'm gwine to tell ye 'bout de ole ark,
De Lord told No-ah for to build him an____ ole ark,

2. Tutti

ole ark, De ole ark a-mov-er-in', a-mov-er-in' a-long,

al rigore di tempo
mp

Oh, de ole ark a-mov-er-in', a-mov-er-in', a-mov-er-in', De

Omit in the last verse

ole ark a-mov-er-in', a-mov-er-in' a-long,

Ole ark a - mov - er - in', a - mov - er - in' a - long.

2

Den Noah an' his sons went to work upon de dry lan',
De ole ark a-moverin', etc.,
Dey built dat ark jes' accordin' to de comman',
De ole ark a-moverin', etc.,
Noah an' his sons went to work upon de timber,
De ole ark a-moverin', etc.,
De proud began to laugh, an' de silly point de'r finger,
De ole ark a-moverin', etc.
Chorus — De ole ark a-moverin', etc.

3

When de ark was finished jes' accordin' to de plan,
De ole ark a-moverin', etc.,
Massa Noah took in his family, both animal an' man,
De ole ark a-moverin', etc.,
When de rain began to fall an' de ark began to rise,
De ole ark a-moverin', etc.,
De wicked hung around wid de'r groans an' de'r cries,
De ole ark a-moverin', etc.
Chorus — De ole ark a-moverin', etc.

4

Forty days an' forty nights, de rain it kep' a fallin',
De ole ark a-moverin', etc.,
De wicked clumb de trees, an' for help dey kep' a callin',
De ole ark a-moverin', etc.,
Dat awful rain, she stopped at last, de waters dey subsided,
De ole ark a-moverin', etc.,
An' dat ole ark wid all on board on Ararat she rided,
De ole ark a-moverin', etc.
Chorus — De ole ark a-moverin', etc.

Hymns on Biblical Themes

Ezekiel Saw de Wheel

E - ze-kiel saw de wheel, 'Way up in de mid-dle ob de air,

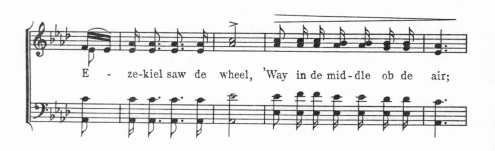

E - ze-kiel saw de wheel, 'Way in de mid-dle ob de air;

An' de lit-tle wheel run by faith, An' de big wheel run by de

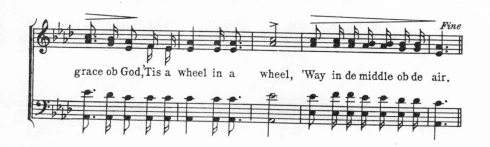

grace ob God,'Tis a wheel in a wheel, 'Way in de middle ob de air.

Solo *quasi extempore sed meme ritmo*
Some go to church fo' to sing an' shout,
Let me tell you what a hypocrit'll do,
One o' dese days, 'bout twelve o'-clock

Tutti *con entusiasmo*

'Way in de middle ob de air;
'Way in de middle ob de air;
'Way in de middle ob de air;

Solo *capriccioso*
Be - fo' six months dey are all turned out,
He'll talk 'bout me an' he'll talk 'bout you,
Dis ole worl' gwine to reel an' rock,

Tutti *D. C.*

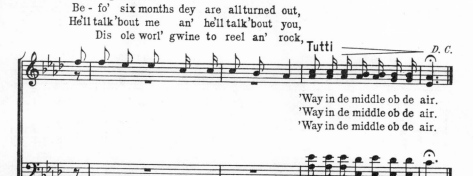

'Way in de middle ob de air.
'Way in de middle ob de air.
'Way in de middle ob de air.

Hymns on Biblical Themes

I Heard the Preaching of the Elder

Moderato ♩ = 72

Refrain *declamato*

poco dim.

I heard the preaching of the el-der, Preaching the Word,

f *poco dim.* *Fine*

preaching the Word; I heard the preaching of the el-der, Preaching the Word of God.

Solo *mf* **Chorus**

How long did it rain? Can an-y one tell? Preaching the Word of

Solo **Chorus** *D. C.*

God; For for-ty— days and nights it fell, Preaching the Word of God.

2

How long was Jonah in the belly of the whale,
  Preaching the Word of God?
For three whole days and nights he sailed,
  Preaching the Word of God.

3

When I was a mourner just like you,
  Preaching the Word of God;
I prayed and prayed till I came through,
  Preaching the Word of God.

Hymns on Biblical Themes

John Saw

2

Mary wept, an' Martha cried – Settin' on, etc.
To see de'r Saviour crucified – Settin' on, etc.
Weepin' Mary, weep no more – Settin' on, etc.
Jesus say He gone before – Settin' on, etc.
Chorus – John saw, etc.

3

Want to go to hebben when I die – Settin' on, etc.
Shout salvation as I fly – Settin' on, etc.
It's a little while longer here below – Settin' on, etc.
Den-a home to glory we shall go – Settin' on, etc.
Chorus – John saw, etc.

Hymns on Biblical Themes

Little David, Play on Your Harp

Un poco allegro ma non troppo ♩ = 92

Refrain
Solo

mf con vita *mf* Tutti *cresc.*

Lit-tle Da - vid, play on ____ your harp, Hal - le - lu'

p Fine

Lit-tle Da - vid, play on ____ your harp, Hal - le - lu'.

Hal - le - lu'

Solo *declamato* *sf* Tutti Solo *declamato* *sf* Tutti Solo

1 God told Mo - ses, O Lord! Go down in-to E - gypt, O Lord!
2 Down in de val-ley, O Lord! Did-n' go ___ t' stay, O Lord! My
3 Come down, an - gels, O Lord! With ink an' ___ pen, ___ O Lord! An'

declamato *sf* Tutti Solo *sf* Tutti D. C.

Tell ole Pha - ro', O Lord! Loose my peo - ple, O Lord!
soul got hap - py, O Lord! I stayed all day, ___ O Lord!
write sal - va - tion, O Lord! To dy - in' men, ___ O Lord!

Hymns on Biblical Themes

My Lord Delibered Daniel

2

Some say dat John de Baptist
　Was nothing but a Jew,
But de Bible doth inform us
　Dat he was a preacher, too;
　　Yes, he was!
Chorus — My Lord delibered Daniel.

3

Oh, Daniel cast in de lions' den,
　He pray both night an' day,
De angel came from Galilee,
　An' lock de lions' jaw.
　　Dat's so!
Chorus — My Lord delibered Daniel.

4

He delibered Daniel from de lions' den,
　Jonah from de belly ob de whale,
And de Hebrew children from de fiery furnace,
　And why not ebery man?
　　Oh, yes!
Chorus — My Lord delibered Daniel.

5

De richest man dat eber I saw
　Was de one dat beg de most,
His soul was filled wid Jesus,
　And wid de Holy Ghost.
　　Yes, it was!
Chorus — My Lord delibered Daniel.

Hymns on Biblical Themes

Oh, He Raise-a Poor Lazarus

(*Bass hum with closed lips*)

2

He give heal unto de sick — yes, He did,
He give sight unto de blin' — I know He did,
   He done 'able de cripple to walk,
    Oh, He raise de dead from under de groun'
    An' give dem permission to talk.

3

Oh, moan along, — moan along,
Oh, ye moanin' souls — ye moanin' souls
   Heaven is my home —
    Jesus been here one time, Lord, He's comin' agin,
    Git ready and let us go home.

Hymns on Biblical Themes

Peter on the Sea

Pe - ter, Pe - ter, Pe - ter on the sea, sea, sea, sea!

Pe - ter, Pe - ter, Pe - ter on the sea, sea, sea, sea!

Pe - ter, Pe - ter, Pe - ter on the sea, sea, sea, sea!

Pe - ter, Pe - ter, Pe - ter on the sea, sea, sea, sea!

Drop your nets and fol - low, Drop your nets and fol - low me.

Drop your nets and fol - low, Drop your nets and fol - low me.

Drop your nets and fol - low, Drop your nets and fol - low me.

Drop your nets and fol - low, Drop your nets and fol - low me.

2
‖: Gabriel, Gabriel, Gabriel, blow your trump, trump, trump, trump! :‖
Gabriel, blow your trumpet, Gabriel, blow your trumpet loud!

3
‖: Daniel, Daniel, Daniel in the lions', lions', :‖
Daniel in the lions', Daniel in the lions' den.

4
‖: Who did, who did, who did swallow Jonah, Jonah? :‖
Who did swallow Jonah, who did swallow Jonah whole?

5
‖: Whale did, whale did, whale did swallow Jonah, Jonah, :‖
Whale did swallow Jonah, whale did swallow Jonah whole!

Hymns on Biblical Themes

'Raslin' Jacob

Moderato fervente ♩ = 76

'Ras-lin' Ja-cob, let me go, 'Ras-lin' Ja-cob, let me go,
'Ras-lin' Ja-cob, let me go, I will not let you go.

Tutti

1 Day is break-in', Ja-cob, let me go, Day is break-in', Ja-cob,
2 If you'll bless my soul, I'll let you go, If you'll bless my soul, I'll
3 When I'm sink-in' down, pit-y me, When I'm sink-in' down,

let me go, Day is break-in', Ja-cob, let me go, I will not let you go.
let you go, If you'll bless my soul, I'll let you go, I will not let you go.
pit-y me, When I'm sink-in' down, pit-y me, I will not let you go.

Hymns on Biblical Themes

See Fo' an' Twenty Elders

Moderato religione ♩ = 72 – 88
Tutti
unison sonore

1 See fo' an' twen-ty el - ders on de'r knees,
2 Dey are bow-in' roun' de al - tar on de'r knees,
3 See Gid-eon's ar - my bow-in' on de'r knees,
4 See Dan-iel 'mong de li - ons on de'r knees,

See___ fo' an' twen-ty el - ders on de'r knees,
Dey___ are bow-in' roun' de al - tar on de'r knees,
See___ Gid-eon's ar - my bow-in' on de'r knees,
See___ Dan-iel 'mong de li - ons on de'r knees,

cresc. *sf*
An' we'll all rise to - ged-der an' view de ri - sin' sun,

sun, O Lord,

più espressivo
O Lord, have mer - cy ef yo' please.

O Lord,

Hymns on Biblical Themes

There Were Ten Virgins

1 And five of them were wise, When, etc.

2 And five of them were foolish, When, etc.

3 And de foolish said to de wise, When, etc.

4 O give us of your oil, When, etc.

5 And de wise said to de foolish, When, etc.

6 O go to them that sell, When, etc.

7 And buy for yourselves, When, etc.

Hymns on Biblical Themes

Wonder Where is Good Ole Daniel

Moderato semplicemente ♩ = 63
Tutti

mp unis

poco cresc. *cresc.*

mf *decresc.* *mp*

1 Won - der where is__ good ole Dan - iel,
2 He was cas' in de den ob li - ons,

Won - der where is_ good ole Dan - iel,_ Won - der where is__
He was cas' in de den ob li - ons,_ He was cas' in de

good ole Dan - iel, Way o - ver in de Prom ise' Lan'.
den ob li - ons, Way o - ver in de Prom ise' Lan'.

3

‖: By an' by we'll go an' meet him, :‖
Way over in de Promise' Lan'.

4

‖: Wonder where's dem Hebrew children, :‖
Way over in de Promise' Lan'.

5

‖: Dey come thro' de fiery furnace, :‖
Way over in de Promise' Lan'.

6

‖: By an' by we'll go an' meet dem, :‖
Way over in de Promise' Lan'.

7

‖: Wonder where is doubtin' Thomas, :‖
Way over in de Promise' Lan'.

8

‖: Wonder where is sinkin' Peter, :‖
Way over in de Promise' Lan'.

Hymns of the Christian Life

I Ain't Goingt' Study War No More

Transcribed by the editor from
the singing of the Hampdon students
led by Paige I. Lancaster

more, Ain't goingt' stud-y war no more, Ain't goingt' stud-y war no

more _____ Ain't goingt' stud-y war no more, Ain't goingt'

Stud-y war no more, I ain't goingt'

stud-y war no more, Ain't goingt' stud-y ____ war no more. ____

2
Going to lay down my burden,
Down by the river side.

3
Going to try on my starry crown,
Down by the river side.

4
Going to meet my dear old father,
Down by the river side.

5
Going to meet my dear old mother,
Down by the river side.

6
Going to meet my loving Jesus,
Down by the river side.

Hymns of the Christian Life

Lord, Until I Reach My Home

Moderato con giusto ♩ = 69

Refrain

Lord, un- **Tutti**

til I reach my home, Un - til I reach my home, I

nev-er 'spect to give the journey o ver, Un - til I reach my home, home.

Solo
recitando

1 Old Sa-tan's might-y bus - y, ___ He fol-lows me night an' day,
2 Now don't you mind old Sa - tan, ___ Wid all ___ his temp-tin' charms,
3 When I was ly-in' at hell's dark door, No one ___ to pit-y poo' me,

An' ___ ev-'ry time I go to pray, I find him in my way.
He ___ wants to steal your soul a-way, An' fol' you in his arms.
Mas-sa Je - sus He come rid-in' by, An' bought my lib-er - ty.

Hymns of the Christian Life

Tell Jesus

Hymns of Christmas
Go Tell It on de Mountain

Moderato, un poco declamando sed espress. ♩=76

Solo

1 When I was a seek-er I sought both night and day, I ask de Lord to help me, An' He show' me de way.

Go tell it on de moun - tain, O - ver de hills an' ev - ry - where; Go tell it on de moun - tain, Dat Je - sus Christ is a - born.

2
He made me a watchman
Upon a city wall,
And if I am a Christian
I am de least of all.
Refrain

*An enclitic retarded and accented at the same time is most unusual; its occurrence here is probably very colloquial. — Editor

Hymns of Christmas

Rise Up, Shepherd, an' Foller

Transcribed by
R. Nathaniel Dett

Moderato un poco declamato ♩ = 80

Solo

1 Dere's a Star in de Eas' on ___ Christ-mas morn,

Tutti * Solo

Rise up, shep-herd, an' fol - ler; It 'll lead to de place where de

3

Sav-iour's born, ___ Rise up, shep-herd, an' fol - ler!

Refrain

Fol - ler, fol - ler, Rise up, shep-herd, an' fol - ler;

più espress. mp

Fol-ler de Star of Beth-le - hem, ___ Rise up, shep-herd, an' fol-ler.

2

If you take good heed to de angel's words,
   Rise up, shepherd, an' foller;
Yo'll forget yo' flocks, yo'll forget yo' herds,
   Rise up, shepherd, an' foller. *Refrain*

* See Appendix for note on flat seventh in Negro music.- Editor

Hymns of the Church
De Church of God

2

Oh, Jesus tole you once before,
To go in peace an' sin no more;
Oh, Paul an' Silas bound in jail,
Den one did sing, an' de oder pray.
Refrain-De church of God, etc.

3

Oh, did you hear my Jesus say
"Come unto me, I am de way?"
Oh, come along, Moses, don't get lost,
Oh, stretch your rod an' come across.
Refrain-De church of God, etc.

Hymns of the Church

'Tis the Ole Ship of Zion

Andante di giusto ♩ = 68

Come a - long, come a - long, and let's go home;

O glo-ry, Hal-le - lu - jah! 'Tis the old ship of Zi - on, Hal-le -

lu - jah, 'Tis the old ship of Zi - on, Ha - le - lu - jah!

2
O what ship is this
That will take us all home?
  O glory, Hallelujah!
Refrain—

3
She has landed many thousand,
And she'll land as many a more.
  O glory, Hallelujah!
Refrain—

4
Do you think she will be able
For to take us all home?
  O glory, Hallelujah!
Refrain—

5
O yes, she will be able
For to take us all home.
  O glory, Hallelujah!
Refrain—

Hymns of Consolation

De Winter'll Soon Be Ober

win-ter, win-ter, de win-ter'll soon be o-ber, chil-dren, Yes, my Lord.

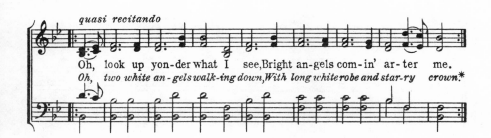

quasi recitando

Oh, look up yon-der what I see, Bright an-gels com-in' ar-ter me.
*Oh, two white an-gels walk-ing down, With long white robe and star-ry crown.**

2

I turn my eyes towards de sky,
An' ask de Lord for wings to fly;
If you get dere before I do,
Look out for me I'm comin' too.

3

Oh, Jordan's ribber is deep an' wide,
But Jesus stan' on de hebbenly side;
An' when we get on Canaan's shore,
We'll shout an' sing forebber more.

*Lines supplied from another folk-hymn, as last half of quatrain was missing. In **Negro** folk-music interchanging of lines or verses from song to song is quite common. —Editor

Hymns of Consolation

Fighting On

Solo

1 Hal - le - lu - jah to the Lamb, Je - sus died for eb - 'ry man.
2 In my room right by my bed, Je - sus take me when I'm dead.

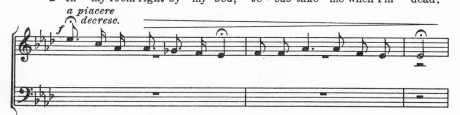

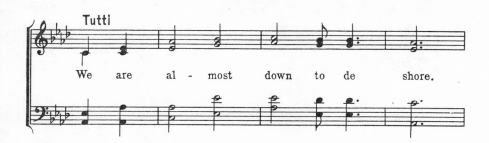

We are al - most down to de shore.

Solo

He died for you, He died for me, He died to save de whole world
When I get on dat oth - er shore, I'll bless my Lord for - ev - er

free.
more.

Tutti

D. C. Refrain

We are al - most down to de shore.

Hymns of Consolation

Most Done Trabelling

Refrain

I'm bound to car-ry my soul to my Je-sus, I'm bound to car-ry my soul to de Lord; Lord.

2
Oh, my sister's in de road,
  Most done trabelling,
My sister's in de road,
  Most done trabelling,
My sister's in de road,
  Most done trabelling.
Chorus — I'm bound to carry, etc.

3
Oh, my brudder's in de road,
  Most done trabelling,
My brudder's in de road,
  Most done trabelling,
My brudder's in de road,
  Most done trabelling.
Chorus — I'm bound to carry, etc.

4
Oh, de preacher's in de road,
  Most done trabelling,
De preacher's in de road,
  Most done trabelling,
De preacher's in de road,
  Most done trabelling.
Chorus — I'm bound to carry, etc.

5
All de member's in de road,
  Most done trabelling,
De member's in de road,
  Most done trabelling,
De member's in de road,
  Most done trabelling.
Chorus — I'm bound to carry, etc.

Hymns of Consolation
There Is a Balm in Gilead

Transcribed from the singing of the
Hampton Institute students by
R. Nathaniel Dett

Andante molto espress ♩ = 60

There is a Balm in Gil-e-ad, To make the wound-ed whole, There is a Balm in Gil-e-ad, To heal the sin-sick soul. There is a soul.

Solo
molto espress.

Some-times I feel dis-cour-aged, And think my work's in vain, But then the Ho-ly Spir-it Re-vives my soul a-gain.

D. C.

2	3
Don't ever be discouraged For Jesus is your friend, And if you lack for knowledge, He'll ne'er refuse to lend.	If you cannot preach like Peter, If you cannot pray like Paul, You can tell the love of Jesus, You can say "He died for all.

Hymns of Consolation

We Are Almost Home

Refrain
Tutti
jiocoso

We are al - most home, We are al - most home, We are al - most home, to ring those charming bells.

1 Oh, come a-long, broth-ers, come a-long, Come a-long, broth-ers, come a-long, Come a-long, broth-ers, come a-long, To ring those charming bells.

2
‖: O come along, sisters, come along,
Come along, sisters, come along,
Come along, sisters, come along,
To ring those charming bells. :‖
Refrain

N. B. Both verse and chorus of this song being sung twice in succession the repeats are to be taken very softly. like echoes. — Editor

Hymns of Death

Good News, de Chariot's Comin'

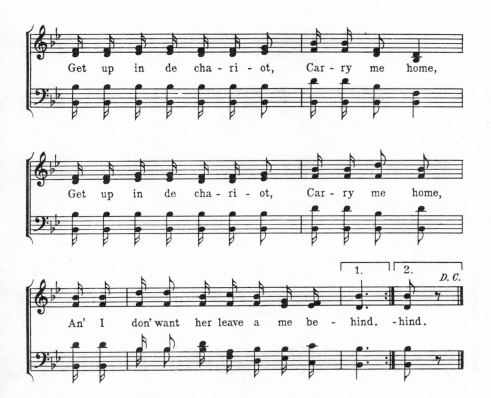

Get up in de cha - ri - ot, Car - ry me home,

Get up in de cha - ri - ot, Car - ry me home,

An' I don' want her leave a me be - hind. -hind.

2

Dar's a long white robe in de hebben, I know,
A long white robe in de hebben, I know,
A long white robe in de hebben, I know,
　An' I don' want her leave-a me behind.
Dar's a golden crown in de hebben, I know,
A golden crown in de hebben, I know,
A golden crown in de hebben, I know,
　An' I don' want her leave-a me behind.
Chorus — Good news, de chariot's comin', etc.

3

Dar's a golden harp in de hebben, I know,
A golden harp in de hebben, I know,
A golden harp in de hebben, I know,
　An' I don' want her leave-a me behind.
Dar's silver slippers in de hebben, I know,
Silver slippers in de hebben, I know,
Silver slippers in de hebben, I know,
　An' I don' want her leave-a me behind.
Chorus — Good news, de chariot's comin', etc.

Hymns of Death

In the Kingdom

Con sentimo sed al rigore di tempo ♩ = 60
Tutti (ritmo a due)
mp

1 My moth - er has gone— to jour - ney a - way,
2 My fa - ther has gone— to jour - ney a - way,
3 My sis - ter has gone— to jour - ney a - way,

My moth - er has gone— to jour - ney a - way,
My fa - ther has gone— to jour - ney a - way,
My sis - ter has gone— to jour - ney a - way,

My moth - er has gone— to jour - ney a - way,
My fa - ther has gone— to jour - ney a - way,
My sis - ter has gone— to jour - ney a - way,

Fine

In the king - dom, in the king - dom to - day.

At Hampton two verses at least are usually sung before proceeding to the chorus. — Editor

Refrain

Hymns of Death

Oh, de Hebben Is Shinin'

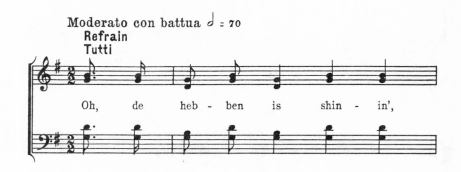

Oh, de heb - ben is shin - in',

shin - in', Oh, Lord, de heb-ben is shin - in' full ob love.

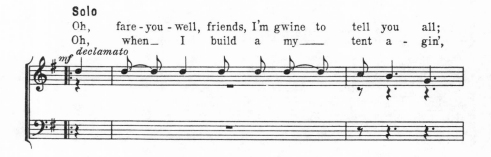

Solo

Oh, fare - you - well, friends, I'm gwine to tell you all;
Oh, when I build a my tent a - gin',

Tutti

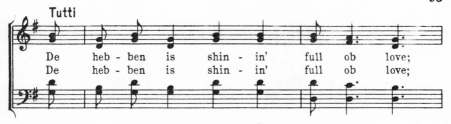

De heb - ben is shin - in' full ob love;
De heb - ben is shin - in' full ob love;

Solo *declamato*

Gwine to leave you all a mine eyes to close;
Build it so ole Sa - tan he can't get in;

Tutti *D. C.*

De heb - ben is shin - in' full ob love.
De heb - ben is shin - in' full ob love.

2

Death say, "I come on a-dat hebbenly 'cree
  De hebben is shinin' full ob love,
My warrant's for to summage thee;
  De hebben is shinin' full ob love,
An' whedder thou prepared or no;
  De hebben is shinin' full ob love,
Dis very day He say you must go;"
  De hebben is shinin' full ob love.
Refrain —

3

Oh, ghastly Death, wouldst thou prevail?
  De hebben is shinin' full ob love,
Oh, spare me yet anoder day;
  De hebben is shinin' full ob love,
I'm but a flower in my bloom;
  De hebben is shinin' full ob love,
Why wilt thou cut-a me down so soon?
  De hebben is shinin' full ob love.
Refrain —

4

Oh, if I had-a my time agin;
  De hebben is shinin' full ob love,
I would hate dat road-a dat leads to sin;
  De hebben is shinin' full ob love,
An' to my God a-wid earnest pray;
  De hebben is shinin' full ob love,
An' wrastle until de break o' day;
  De hebben is shinin' full ob love.
Refrain —

Hymns of Death

Oh, Give Way, Jordan

Duet

An' I wish dat mu - sic would __ come here,
An' I wish dat mu - sic would __ come here,

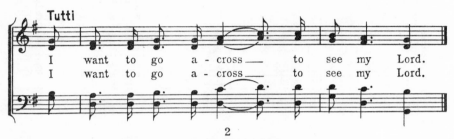

Tutti

I want to go a - cross __ to see my Lord.
I want to go a - cross __ to see my Lord.

2

Oh, stow back, stow back de powers of hell,
    I want to go across to see my Lord,
And let God's children take de field,
    I want to go across to see my Lord,
Now stan' back Satan, let me go by,
    I want to go across to see my Lord,
Gwine to serve my Jesus till I die,
    I want to go across to see my Lord.
Refrain—

3

Soon in de mornin' by de break ob day,
    I want to go across to see my Lord,
See de ole ship ob Zion sailin' away,
    I want to go across to see my Lord,
Now I must go across, an' I shall go across,
    I want to go across to see my Lord,
Dis sinful world I count but dross,
    I want to go across to see my Lord.
Refrain—

4

Oh, I heard such a lumberin' in de sky,
    I want to go across to see my Lord,
It make a-me t'ink my time was nigh,
    I want to go across to see my Lord,
Yes, it must be my Jesus in de cloud,
    I want to go across to see my Lord,
I nebber heard him speak so loud,
    I want to go across to see my Lord.
Refrain—

Hymns of Death

Oh, Wasn't Dat a Wide Riber?

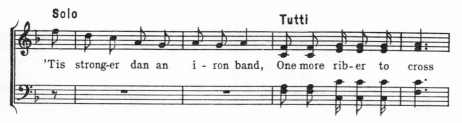

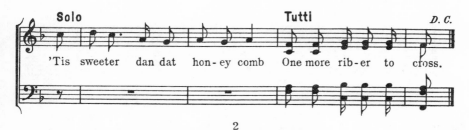

2

Oh, de good ole chariot passing by,
  One more riber to cross,
She jarred de earth an' shook de sky,
  One more riber to cross.
I pray, good Lord, shall I be one?
  One more riber to cross,
To get up in de chariot, trabbel on,
  One more riber to cross.
Chorus—Oh, wasn't dat a wide riber? etc.

3

We're told dat de fore-wheel run by love,
  One more riber to cross,
We're told dat de hind-wheel run by faith,
  One more riber to cross.
I hope I shall get dere bimeby,
  One more riber to cross,
To jine de number in de sky,
  One more riber to cross.
Chorus—Oh, wasn't dat a wide riber? etc.

4

Oh, one more riber we hab to cross,
  One more riber to cross,
'Tis Jordan's riber we hab to cross,
  One more riber to cross.
Oh, Jordan's riber am chilly an' cold,
  One more riber to cross,
But I got de glory in-a my soul,
  ·One more riber to cross.
Chorus—Oh, wasn't dat a wide riber? etc.

Hymns of Death

Swing Low, Chariot

Moderato con entusiasma ♩ = 72

Solo

1 Swing low, char-i-ot, low in de Eas', Let God's peo-ple
2 Swing low, char-i-ot, low in de Wes', Let God's peo-ple
3 Swing low, char-i-ot, low in de North, Let God's peo-ple
4 Swing low, char-i-ot, low in de South, Let God's peo-ple

Tutti

have some peace, Gwine t' ride in de char-i-ot in de morn-in',
have some res', Gwine t' ride in de char-i-ot in de morn-in',
have a talk, Gwine t' ride in de char-i-ot in de morn-in',
have a shout, Gwine t' ride in de char-i-ot in de morn-in',

Solo   Tutti

Swing low— Gwine t' ride in de char-i-ot in de morn-in',

Solo   Tutti   Repeat pp

E-li-jah, Gwine t' ride in de char-i-ot in de morn-in'.

Hymns of Death

Swing Low, Sweet Chariot

2
Oh, de good ole chariot will take us home,
I don't want to leave me behind.
Chorus — Oh, swing low, sweet chariot, etc.

Hymns of Death
Swing Low, Sweet Chariot

Transcribed by
R. Nathaniel Dett
from the singing of the
Hampton students

Lento con molto espressione ♩ = 56

If you get there before I do,
  Coming for to carry me home,
Tell all my friends I'm coming too;
  Coming for to carry me home.

I'm sometimes up, I'm sometimes down,
  Coming for to carry me home,
But still my soul feels heavenly bound;
  Coming for to carry me home.

But He Ain't Comin' Here t' Die No Mo'

Adagio gravemente ♩ = 60

Refrain
Tutti

But He ain't com - in' here t' die no mo', ____ Ain't com-in' here t' die no mo'. ____

Solo**
narrante tempo rubato ____ *rit. un poco*

1 Vir-gin Ma-ry had one Son, The cru-el Jews had him hung.

2	4
Hallelujah t' de Lamb, Jesus died for every man. But He ain't comin' here t' die no mo', Ain't comin' here t' die no mo'.	He died for de rich, He died for de po' He ain't comin' here t' die no mo', But He ain't comin' here t' die no mo', Ain't comin' here t' die no mo'.

3	5
He died for yo' He died for me, He died t' set po' sinner free. But He ain't comin' here t' die no mo', Ain't comin' here t' die no mo'.	He died for de blind, He died for de lame, He bore de pain an' all de blame. But He ain't comin' here t' die no mo', Ain't comin' here t' die no mo'.

* Omit this last measure when refrain is to be followed by a verse.

**This solo is frequently sung thus:—

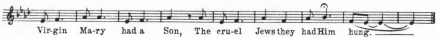

Vir-gin Ma-ry had a Son, The cru-el Jews they had Him hung. ____

Hymns of the Death of Christ

Did You Hear How Dey Crucified My Lord?

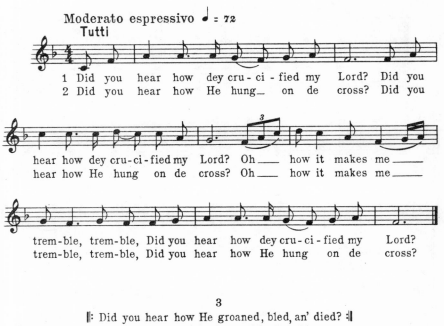

Moderato espressivo ♩ = 72
Tutti

1 Did you hear how dey cru-ci-fied my Lord? Did you
2 Did you hear how He hung― on de cross? Did you

hear how dey cru-ci-fied my Lord? Oh―― how it makes me――
hear how He hung on de cross? Oh―― how it makes me――

trem-ble, trem-ble, Did you hear how dey cru-ci-fied my Lord?
trem-ble, trem-ble, Did you hear how He hung on de cross?

3
‖: Did you hear how He groaned, bled, an' died? :‖
Oh, how it makes me tremble, tremble,
Did you hear how He groaned, bled, an' died?

4
‖: Did you hear how dey laid Him in de tomb? :‖
Oh, how it makes me tremble, tremble,
Did you hear how dey laid Him in de tomb?

5
‖: Did you hear how He rose from de grave? :‖
Oh, how it makes me tremble, tremble,
Did you hear how He rose from de grave?

The version "Were You There When They Crucified My Lord" seems to be universally more popular.

Hymns of the Death of Christ
My Soul Wants Something That's New

Andante quasi meditatione ♩. = 69

Solo *mp* ——————— *mf* **Tutti**

My soul wants some-thing that's new, that's new, My

poco cresc.

soul wants some-thing that's new,— My soul wants some-thing that's

poco dim. *Fine*

new, that's new,— My soul wants some-thing that's new.—

Solo *meno tempo mp* ——————— *mf* **Tutti**

1 Dark was the night and cold the ground, On which the Lord was
2 Was it for crimes that I had done, He groaned up-on— the

poco cresc. *poco dim.* *D. C.*

laid, His sweat like drops of blood run down, In ag-o-ny He prayed.
tree? A-maz-ing pi-ty, grace un-known, And love be-yond de-gree.

Hymns of the Death of Christ

Were You There When They Crucified My Lord?

Transcribed by
R. Nathaniel Dett*

2 Were you there when they nailed Him to the tree?

3 Were you there when they pierced Him in the side?

4 Were you there when the sun refused to shine?

5 Were you there when they laid Him in the tomb?

*The effort here has been to transcribe the effect of the thousand voices of the school in which there are numerous parts. A little study reveals the fact that these parts are so very simple and natural that no group of singers should be daunted by them. — Editor

Hymns of Deliverance

Children, We All Shall Be Free

From the collection of
R. Nathaniel Dett

* "In his soul" is traditional; however, because of the rhyme, "in his view", suggests itself —Editor

Hymns of Deliverance

Go Down, Moses

Transcribed by the editor from
the singing of the Hampton students
led by Paige I. Lancaster

Moderato molto maestoso ♩ = 72

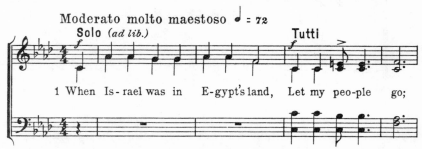

1 When Is-rael was in E-gypt's land, Let my peo-ple go;

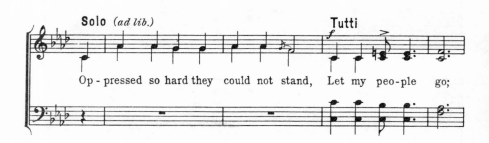

Op-pressed so hard they could not stand, Let my peo-ple go;

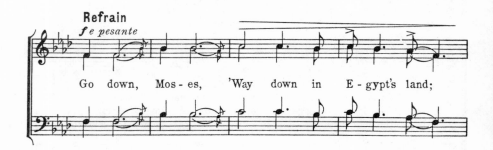

Go down, Mos-es, 'Way down in E-gypt's land;

Tell ole Pha - raoh __ Let my peo - ple go.

2

Thus saith the Lord, bold Moses said,
   Let my people go;
If not I'll smite your first-born dead,
   Let my people go.

3

No more shall they in bondage toil,
   Let my people go;
Let them come out with Egypt's spoil,
   Let my people go.

4

The Lord told Moses what to do,
   Let my people go;
To lead the children of Israel thro',
   Let my people go.

5

When they had reached the other shore,
   Let my people go;
They sang a song of triumph o'er.
   Let my people go.

At Hampton Institute the first two measures of the last score are sung as here indicated, and while this is undoubtedly a colloquialism it, nevertheless, is highly effective. — Editor

Tell __ ole Pha - raoh

Hymns of Deliverance

Oh, Freedom!

3	5
No mo' weepin' over me, An' befo' I'd be a slave, I'll be buried in my grave, An' go home to my Lord an' be free.	There'll be shoutin' over me, An' befo' I'd be a slave, I'll be buried in my grave, An' go home to my Lord an' be free.
4	**6**
There'll be singin' over me, An' befo' I'd be a slave, I'll be buried in my grave, An' go home to my Lord an' be free.	There'll be prayin' over me, An' befo' I'd be a slave, I'll be buried in my grave, An' go home to my Lord an' be free.

Hymns of Deliverance

Steal Away to Jesus

Transcribed by
R. Nathaniel Dett

Andante assai, con molto espress. ♩ = 60

Refrain

Steal a-way, steal a-way, Steal a-way to Je-sus;

tempo rubato poco rit.

Fine

Steal a-way, steal a-way home, I ain't got long to stay here.

Solo

ff con molto espressione

1 My Lord— calls me, He calls me by the thun-der;
2 Green trees are bend-ing, Poor sin-ner stands a-trembling;
3 Tomb-stones are burst-ing, Poor sin-ner stands a-trembling; The trumpet sounds with-
4 My Lord— calls me, He calls me by the light-ning;

molto morendo

Tutti

rit. *a tempo D. S.*

in-a my soul, I ain't got long to stay here. Steal a-way, steal a-way.

* The flat is not always distinctly heard in the Hampton chorus — Editor

Hymns of Deliverance

Slav'ry Chain

Sung by
Mrs. Catharine Fields-Gay

Collected by
R. Nathaniel Dett

Giocoso ♩ = 88

Tutti Refrain

Slav'ry chain done broke at las', broke at las', ___ broke at las',

1st and last verse / after other verses

Slav'ry chain done broke at las', Goin' to praise God 'til I die. die. ___

1 'Way up in-a dat val-ley, ___ Pray-in' on my knees; ___

con espress. *Refrain*

Tellin' God ___ a-bout my trou-bles, An' to he'p me ef-a He please.

Solo

2 I did tell Him how I suf-fer ___ In de
4 I done 'pint one might-y cap-tain ___ For to

dun-geon an' de chain; ___ An' de days I went wif
mar-shall all my hosts; ___ An' to bring my bleed-ing

D. C. Refrain

head bowed down, An' my bro-ken flesh an' ___ pain, (But breth-er-en)
ones to me An' ___ not one shall be ___ lost.

Solo

3 I did know my Je-sus heard me ___ 'Cause de
5 Now no more wear-y trav'-lin' ___ 'Cause my

spir-it spoke to me ___ An' said "Rise my chile, your
Je-sus set-a me free ___ An' dere's no more auct-ion

Refrain

chill-un An' ___ you too shall ___ be free".
block for me Since He give me lib-er-ty.

Hymns of Encouragement

Don't Be Weary, Traveller

Don't be wea-ry, trav-el-ler, Come a-long home to Je-sus,

Don't be wea-ry, trav-el-ler, Come a-long home to Je-sus.

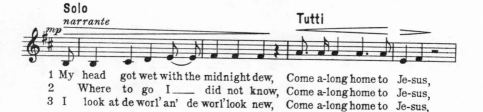

1 My head got wet with the midnight dew, Come a-long home to Je-sus,
2 Where to go I___ did not know, Come a-long home to Je-sus,
3 I look at de worl' an' de worl' look new, Come a-long home to Je-sus,

An-gels bear me wit-ness too, Come a-long home to Je-sus.
Ev-er since He freed my soul, Come a-long home to Je-sus.
I look at my hands an' they look so too, Come a-long home to Je-sus.

Hymns of Encouragement

Don't Get Weary

2

Oh, whar you runnin', sinner?
  I do love de Lord—
De judgment day is a-comin'!
  I do love de Lord.
Chorus — My bretheren, etc.

3

You'll see de world on fire!
  I do love de Lord—
You'll see de element a-meltin',
  I do love de Lord.
Chorus — My bretheren, etc.

4

You'll see de moon a-bleedin',
  I do love de Lord—
You'll see de stars a-fallin';
  I do love de Lord.
Chorus — My bretheren, etc.

Hymns of Encouragement
We Are Building on a Rock

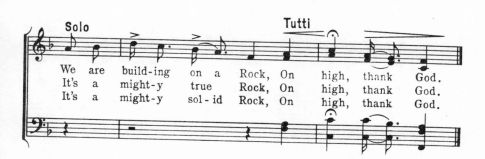

4

Christ Jesus is the Rock,
  On high, on high,
Christ Jesus is the Rock,
  On high, thank God.

5

The very gates of hell,
  On high, on high,
The very gates of hell,
  On high, thank God.

6

Will not 'gainst it prevail,
  On high, on high,
Will not 'gainst it prevail,
  On high, thank God.

7

Help me build on the Rock,
  On high, on high,
Help me build on the Rock,
  On high, thank God.

Hymns of Encouragement

We Are Walking in de Light*

*From Tuskegee Collection, by permission·

*At Hampton Institute these verses are sung very freely with pauses (largely at the impulse of the singer) on the words as indicated.— Editor

Hymns of Encouragement

We Are Climbing Jacob's Ladder

Andante ♩ = 66
Tutti

1 We are climbing Jacob's ladder, We are climbing Jacob's ladder, We are climbing Jacob's ladder, Sol-dier of the cross.

2
Every round goes higher and higher,
Soldier of the cross.

3
Sinner, do you love my Jesus?
Soldier of the cross.

4
If you love Him, why not serve Him?
Soldier of the cross.

5
Do you think I'd make a soldier?
Soldier of the cross.

6
We are climbing higher and higher,
Soldier of the cross.

Hymns of the Faith and Fellowship

Don't Call de Roll

Hymns of the Faith and Fellowship

I Am Goin' to Join in This Army

Moderato resoluto ♩=76

Tutti

mf

I am go-in' to join in this ar-my of my Lord,

I am go-in' to join in this ar - my.

Fine

Solo *semplice*   **Tutti**

1 Takes a hum-ble soul to join, In this ar-my of my Lord,
2 All Chris-tians can join, In this ar-my of my Lord,
3 Preach-er, help us to join, In this ar-my of my Lord,

Solo *semplice*   **Tutti**   *D. C.*

Takes a hum-ble soul to join, In this ar - my.
All Chris-tians can join, In this ar - my.
Preach-er, help us to join, In this ar - my.

Hymns of the Faith and Fellowship

I'll Be There in the Morning*

Moderato ♩ = 72
Refrain
più cresc.

I'll be there in the morning, I'll be there in the morn-ing, I'll be there in the morn-ing.

1st and 4th Verses
When the gen'ral roll is called, When the gen'ral roll is called, Yes, I'll be there; Gwine to pray with Hez-e-kiah, Yes, I'll be there; Gwine to sing with Jer-e-miah, I'll be there; Yes, I'll be there.

To Refrain

2
When the gen'ral roll is called,
Yes, I'll be there;
Gwine to sing around the throne,
Yes, I'll be there;
Gwine to pray around the throne,
Yes, I'll be there;
Gwine to wear a white robe,
Yes, I'll be there.

3
When the gen'ral roll is called,
Yes, I'll be there;
Gwine to see my Massa Jesus,
Yes, I'll be there;
Gwine to wear a starry crown,
Yes, I'll be there;
Gwine to live for evermore,
Yes, I'll be there.

* From Tuskegee Collection, by permission
** End the last verse at this note.

Hymns of the Faith and Fellowship

I'm Gwine to Jine de Great 'Sociation

"This was sung by a boy who was sold down South by his master; and when he parted from his mother, these were the words he sang."—J. H. Bailey

2 I'm gwine to climb up Jacob's ladder,

3 I'm gwine to climb up higher and higher,

4 I'm gwine to sit down at the welcome table,

5 I'm gwine to feast off milk and honey,

6 I'm gwine to tell God how-a you sarved me,

7 I'm gwine to jine de big baptizin',

Den my little soul's gwine to shine, shine

Den my little soul's gwine to shine along

Hymns of the Faith and Fellowship

I've Got a Mother in de Heaven

Hymns of the Future Life

By and By

Transcribed by the editor from
the singing of the Hampton students
led by Paige I. Lancaster

2

O hell is a deep and dark despair,
I'm goin' to lay down this heavy load,
So stop, poor sinner, and don't go there,
I'm goin' to lay down this heavy load.

3

O when I get to heav'n goin' to sing and shout,
I'm goin' to lay down this heavy load,
For there's no one there for to turn me out,
I'm goin' to lay down this heavy load.

4

O Christians, can't you rise and tell,
I'm goin' to lay down this heavy load,
That Jesus hath done all things well,
I'm goin' to lay down this heavy load.

Hymns of the Future Life

Goin' to Shout All Over God's Heav'n

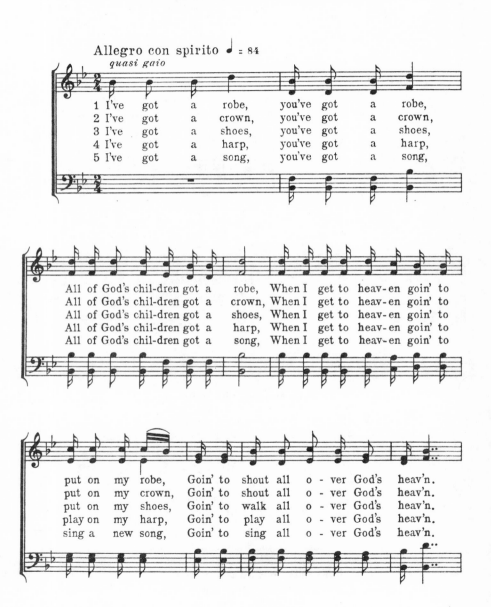

Refrain

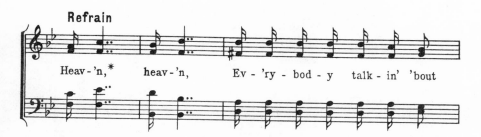

Heav-'n,* heav-'n, Ev - 'ry - bod - y talk - in' 'bout

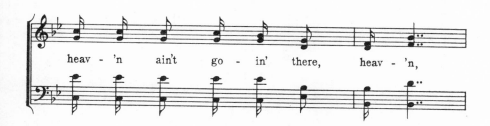

heav - 'n ain't go - in' there, heav - 'n,

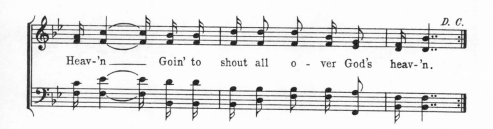

D. C.

Heav-'n ____ Goin' to shout all o - ver God's heav-'n.

Ending for last stanza
p

Repeat pendosi

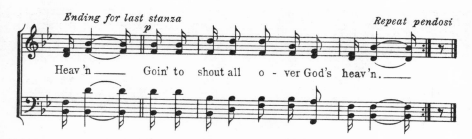

Heav 'n ____ Goin' to shout all o - ver God's heav'n. ____

*Let the last syllable of "Heav'n" be a hum.

Hymns of the Future Life
Oh, When I Git t' Heaven

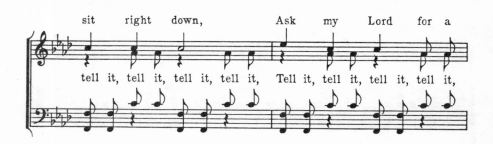

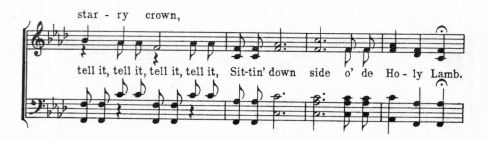

Not a familiar song at Hampton; the version entitled "Father Abraham" is more used. — Ed.

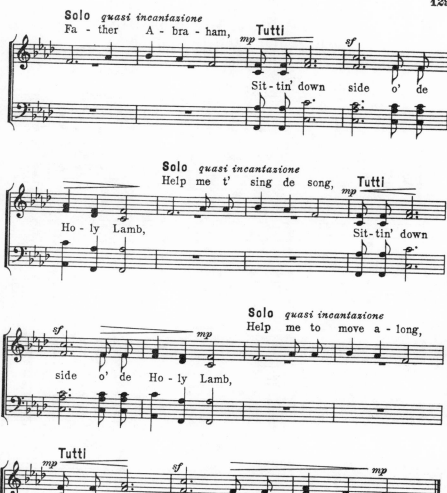

2
Oh, when I git t' Heaven gwine t' sit an' tell,
Three archangels gwine t' ring dem bell,
Sittin' down side o' de Holy Lamb.
Refrain

3
Oh, when I git t' Heaven gwine t' ease, ease,
Me an' my God gwine t' do as we please,
Sittin' down side o' de Holy Lamb.
Refrain

Hymns of the Future Life
In That Beautiful World on High

This was sung by the hands in Mayo's Tobacco Factory, Richmond, and was originally called
"The Mayo Boys' Song." — *Thomas P. Fenner*

I hope my sister will be there,
In that beautiful world on high,
That used to join with me in prayer,
In that beautiful world on high.
Refrain — Oh, I will be there, etc.

I hope my brother will be there,
In that beautiful world on high,
That used to join with me in prayer,
In that beautiful world on high.
Refrain — Oh, I will be there, etc.

4

I know my Saviour will be there,
In that beautiful world on high,
That used to listen to my prayer,
In that beautiful world on high.
Refrain — Oh, I will be there, etc.

Hymns of Invitation

Git on Board, Little Children

Git on board, lit-tle chil-dren, Git on board, lit-tle chil-dren,

Git on board, lit-tle chil-dren, Dere's room for man-y a mo'.

Solo

1 De Gos - pel train's a - com-in', I hear it jus' at han',
2 I hear de train a - com-in', She's com-in' roun' de curve,
3 De fare is cheap an' all can go, De rich an' poor are dere,

I hear de car wheels rum - blin', An' roll - in' thro' de lan'.
She's loos-ened all her steam an' brakes, An' strain-in' eb-'ry nerve.
No sec-ond class a - board dis train, No dif-f'rence in de fare.

Hymns of Invitation

Come Down, Sinner

Moderato affetuoso ♩ = 72
Refrain
Tutti

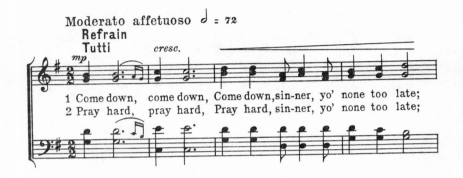

1 Come down, come down, Come down, sin-ner, yo' none too late;
2 Pray hard, pray hard, Pray hard, sin-ner, yo' none too late;

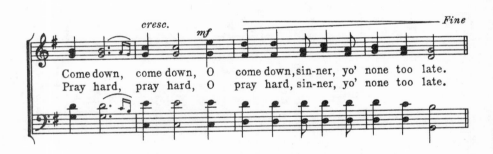

Come down, come down, O come down, sin-ner, yo' none too late.
Pray hard, pray hard, O pray hard, sin-ner, yo' none too late.

Solo
quasi extempore   Tutti

Some seek de Lord, but doan seek Him right, Come down, sinner, yo' none too late;
Times ain't like dey used to ___ be, Come down, sinner, yo' none too late;

Lil' at de day an' none at night; Come down, sinner, yo' none too late.
I __ fo' __ yo' an' yo' fo' me; Come down, sinner, yo' none too late.

3

‖: Bow low, bow low,
  Bow low, sinner, yo' none too late; :‖
Wen' down de hill t' say my prayer,
  Come down, sinner, yo' none too late;
When I got dere, ole Satan was dere,
  Come down, sinner, yo' none too late.

4

‖: Seek hard, seek hard,
  Seek hard, sinner, yo' none too late; :‖
What do yo' tink ole Satan say?
  Come down, sinner, yo' none too late;
"Jesus dead, an' God gone away,"
  Come down, sinner, yo' none too late.

5

‖: Shout hard, shout hard,
  Shout hard, sinner, yo' none too late; :‖
What t' do, I did not know,
  Come down, sinner, yo' none too late;
Right back home I had to go,
  Come down, sinner, yo' none too late.

6

‖: Mourn hard, mourn hard,
  Mourn hard, sinner, yo' none too late; :‖
Something spoke unto my soul,
  Come down, sinner, yo' none too late;
"Go in peace, an' sin no mo',"
  Come down, sinner, yo' none too late.

Hymns of Invitation
Ef You Want to Get to Hebben

Allegretto con grazia ♩ = 72

Solo

Ef you want to get to hebben,
Ef you want to see de an-gels, **Tutti**

come a - long, come a - long, Ef you
come a - long, come a - long, Ef you

want to get to heb - ben, come a - long, come a - long, Ef you
want to see de an - gels, come a - long, come a - long, Ef you

want to get to heb - ben, come a - long, come a - long,
want to see de an - gels, come a - long, come a - long,

Refrain
Jubilate
mf

Hear my Je-sus when He call you. Did you hear my Je-sus when He
Hear my Je-sus when He call you.

cresc.

call you, Did you hear my Je-sus when He call you, Did you

hear my Je-sus when He call you, For to try on your long white robe? robe?

2

Oh, de hebben gates are open, come along, come along,
Oh, de hebben gates are open, come along, come along, *(bis)*
   Hear my Jesus when He call you;
Oh, my mother's in de kingdom, come along, come along,
Oh, my mother's in de kingdom, come along, come along, *(bis)*
   Hear my Jesus when He call you;
I am gwine to meet her yander, come along, come along,
I am gwine to meet her yander, come along, come along, *(bis)*
   Hear my Jesus when He call you.
Chorus – Did you hear my Jesus when He call you,
      Did you hear my Jesus when He call you, *(bis)*
        For to try on your long white robe?

3

Ef you want to wear de slippers, come along, come along,
Ef you want to wear de slippers, come along, come along, *(bis)*
   Hear my Jesus when He call you;
Ef you want to lib forever, come along, come along,
Ef you want to lib forever, come along, come along, *(bis)*
   Hear my Jesus when He call you;
Did you hear my Jesus calling, "Come along, come along,"
Did you hear my Jesus calling, "Come along, come along," *(bis)*
   Hear my Jesus when He call you.
Chorus – Did you hear my Jesus when He call you,
      Did you hear my Jesus when He call you, *(bis)*
        For to try on your long white robe?

Hymns of Invitation

Listen to de Lambs

Solo

1 Come on, sis - ter, with your ups an' downs,
2 Come on, sis - ter, an' a - don't be 'shame,
3 Mind out, broth - er, how you walk de cross,

declamato

Want to go to heav - en when I die;
Want to go to heav - en when I die;
Want to go to heav - en when I die;

Solo

An - gels wait - ing for to give you a crown,—
An - gels wait - ing for to write your— name,—
Foot might slip— an' your soul get— lost,—

Tutti

Want to go to heav - en when I die. •O
Want to go to heav - en when I die. O
Want to go to heav - en when I die. O

D. C.

Hymns of Invitation

View de Land

Moderato animato ♩ = 96

Refrain

Oh, 'way o - ver Jer - dan, View de land, View de land,

'Way o - ver Jer - dan, Go view de heav'n-ly land, Oh, land.

Solo   Tutti

I'm born_ of_ God, I know I am, View de land; View de land;
I want to go to Heav-en when I die, View de land; View de land;

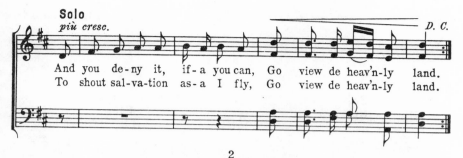

Solo
più cresc.   *D. C.*

And you de-ny it,   if- a you can,   Go   view de heav'n-ly   land.
To shout sal-va-tion as- a I fly,   Go   view de heav'n-ly   land.

2

What kind o' shoes is dem-a you wear,
   View de land, view de land,
Dat you can walk upon de air?
   Go view de heav'nly land,
Dem shoes I wear am de gospel shoes,
   View de land, view de land,
An' you can wear dem ef-a you choose;
   Go view de heav'nly land.
Refrain — Oh, way over, etc.

3

Dere is a tree in Paradise,
   View de land, view de land,
De Christian he call it de tree ob life;
   Go view de heav'nly land,
I spects to eat de fruit right off o' dat tree,
   View de land, view de land,
Ef busy old Satan will let-a me be;
   Go view de heav'nly land.
Refrain — Oh, way over, etc.

4

You say yer Jesus set-a you free,
   View de land, view de land,
Why don't you let-a your neighbor be?
   Go view de heav'nly land,
You say you're aiming for de skies,
   View de land, view de land,
Why don't you stop-a your telling lies?
   Go view de heav'nly land.
Refrain — Oh, way over, etc.

N B Where the vocal range permits the solo is sometimes sung to this melody for the first two
measure of each score

Hymns of Invitation

What Yo' Gwine t' Do When de Lamp Burn Down?

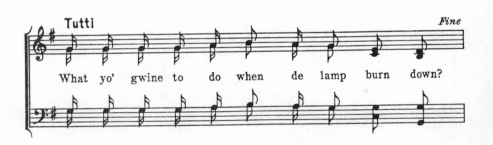

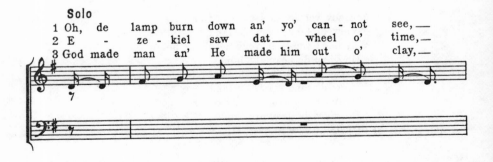

Oh, de
An'___
An' put

Tutti

What yo' gwine t' do when de lamp burn down?
What yo' gwine t' do when de lamp burn down?
What yo' gwine t' do when de lamp burn down?

lamp burn down an' yo' can - not see;___
ev - 'ry spoke was of hu - man kind;___
him on de earth, but not to stay;___

Tutti   *D. C.*

What yo' gwine t' do when de lamp burn down?
What yo' gwine t' do when de lamp burn down?
What yo' gwine t' do when de lamp burn down?

4

Dey cast ole Daniel in de lions' den,
What yo' gwine t' do when de lamp burn down?
An' Jesus locked de lions' jaw;
What yo' gwine t' do when de lamp burn down?
Refrain—

5

Ole Satan's mad an' I am glad;
What yo' gwine t' do when de lamp burn down?
He miss one soul he thought he had;
What yo' gwine t' do when de lamp burn down?
Refrain—

6

Ole Satan's a liar an' a conjurer too,
What yo' gwine t' do when de lamp burn down?
If yo' don't mind, he slip it on yo';
What yo' gwine t' do when de lamp burn down?
Refrain—

Hymns of Invitation

Who'll Jine de Union?

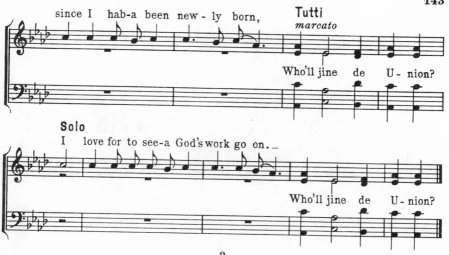

2

Ef ye want to ketch-a dat hebbenly breeze,
  Who'll jine de Union?
Go down in de valley upon yer knees,
  Who'll jine de Union?
Go bend yer knees right smoove wid de groun',
  Who'll jine de Union?
An' pray to de Lord to turn you roun',
  Who'll jine de Union?
Refrain- Oh, Hallelujah, etc.

3

Say, ef you belong to de Union ban',
  Who'll jine de Union?
Den here's my heart, an' here's my han',
  Who'll jine de Union?
I love yer all, both bond an' free,
  Who'll jine de Union?
I love you ef-a you don't love me,
  Who'll jine de Union?
Refrain- Oh, Hallelujah, etc.

4

Now ef you want to know ob me,
  Who'll jine de Union?
Jess who I am, an' a-who I be,
  Who'll jine de Union?
I'm a chile ob God, wid my soul sot free,
  Who'll jine de Union?
For Christ hab bought my liberty,
  Who'll jine de Union?
Refrain- Oh, Hallelujah, etc.

Hymns of Invitation

Somebody's Knocking at Your Door

Hymns of Jesus Christ

He's the Lily of the Valley

Moderato ♩ = 80

1 He's the lil-y of the val-ley, Oh, my Lord; He's the lil-y of the val-ley, Oh, my Lord. King Je-sus in His chariot rides, Oh, my Lord; With four white horses side by side, Oh, my Lord.

2

What kind of shoes are those you wear,
   Oh, my Lord;
That you can ride upon the air?
   Oh, my Lord.
Chorus — He's the lily, etc.

3

These shoes I wear are gospel shoes,
   Oh, my Lord;
And you can wear them if you choose,
   Oh, my Lord.
Chorus — He's the lily, etc.

Hymns of Jesus Christ

He Is King of Kings

Moderato maestoso molto sonoro ♩ = 76

Refrain

Solo — He is / Tutti — King of kings, / Solo — He is / Tutti — Lord of lords.

Je - sus Christ, first and last, No man works like Him. *Fine*

Solo *recitando* — *mf*

1 He built a plat-form in the air,— No man works like Him;
2 He pitched a tent on Ca-naan's ground, No man works like Him;
3 I know that my Re-deem-er lives, No man works like Him;

Tutti

Solo — Tutti — *D. C.*

He meets the saints from ev - 'ry - where; No man works like Him.
And broke the Ro - man kingdom down; No man works like Him.
And by His death sweet blessings gives; No man works like Him.

Hymns of Jesus Christ
King Emanuel

2

Oh, some call Him Jesus; but I call Him Lord,
    I call my Jesus King Emanuel.
Let's talk about de hebben an' de hebben's fine t'ings,
    I call my Jesus King Emanuel.
Refrain — Oh, de King Emanuel, etc.

3

Oh, steady, steady, a little while;
    I call my Jesus King Emanuel.
I will tell you what my Lord done for me;
    I call my Jesus King Emanuel.
Refrain — Oh, de King Emanuel, etc.

4

He pluck-a my feet out de miry clay;
    I call my Jesus King Emanuel.
He sot dem-a on de firm Rock o' Age;
    I call my Jesus King Emanuel.
Refrain — Oh, de King Emanuel, etc.

Hymns of Jesus Christ
Ride on, Jesus

Arranged by the editor from the
recording and transcribing of this song
by Natalie Curtis Burlin after
the singing of the Hampton Quartet

Solo
declamato

1 Ef yo' see my moth-er, _____
2 Ef yo' see my fa - ther, _____
3 Ef yo' see my sis - ter, _____
4 Ef yo' see my broth-er, _____

Jes' tell her fo' me _____ fo' t'
(him)

Tutti

O yes! O yes!

meet me t'-mor-row in Gal-i-lee; Want t' go t' heb-b'n in de mo'n-in'. O

Want t' go t' heb-b'n in de mo'n-in'.

**Tutti as
before   Solo**

5 Ef yo' see John de Bap-tis', O yes! Jes' tell him for me,
6 Ef yo' want t' go t' heb-b'n, O yes! Well, I'll tell yo' how,

Tutti   Solo

O yes! Dat I's been to de rib-ber an I's been bap-tized;
O yes! Jes__ keep yo'__ han's on de gos-pel plow;

Tutti   Solo

Want t' go t' heb-b'n in de mo'n - in'. O

Hymns of Jesus Christ

My Lord's a-Riding All the Time*

2

Come down, come down, my Lord, come down,
　My Lord's a-riding all the time;
And take me up to wear the crown,
　My Lord's a-riding all the time.

3

O sinner, you had better pray,
　My Lord's a-riding all the time;
It looks like judgment ebery day,
　My Lord's a-riding all the time.

*This song originally came to Hampton Institute from Fisk University. What variations our students have evolved can be seen by comparison with the Fisk edition — Editor

Hymns of Jesus Christ
Why, He's the Lord of Lords*

Moderato decisivo ♩ = 80

Why, He's the Lord of lords, And the King of kings, Why,

Je - sus Christ is the first and the last, No one can work like Him.

Solo *(ad lib.)*

Tutti *(ad lib.)*

Solo *(ad lib.)*

I will not let you go, my Lord, No one can work like Him; Un -

Tutti *(ad lib.)*

til you come and bless my soul, No one can work like Him.

2
For Paul and Silas bound in jail,
  No one can work like Him;
The Christians prayed both night and day,
  No one can work like Him.
Chorus—Why, He's the Lord, etc.

3
I wish those mourners would believe,
  No one can work like Him;
That Jesus is ready to receive,
  No one can work like Him.
Chorus—Why, He's the Lord, etc.

* Fisk Jubilee Collection, by permission

Hymns of Judgment

Going to Heaven

♩ = 72
Solo
mf recitando

1 {De book of rev - e - la - tion God to us re-vealed, De
De way de book was o-pened John plain-ly in-formed, De

mys - t'ries of sal - va - tion De book of sev - en seals.}
law of God was brok - en, A Sav - iour must be born.

Refrain
Solo
cresc.

Tutti

Going to heav - en, going to heav - en, Going to

Fine

Heav - en to see that bleed - ing Lamb.

2

John saw de heavens open,
  De Conqueror riding down,
He looked and saw white horses,
  And rider following on.
If you want to know de Conqueror,
  He is de Word of God,
His eyes are like a burnin' throne,
  He is de Word of God. — *Refrain*

3

Hosanna to de Prince of Life,
  Who clothed Himself in clay,
And entered de iron gate of death,
  And bore de ties away.
See how de Conqueror mounts aloft,
  And to His Father flies!
With scars of honor on His flesh,
  And trials in His eyes. — *Refrain*

Hymns of Judgment

Go, Mary, an' Toll de Bell

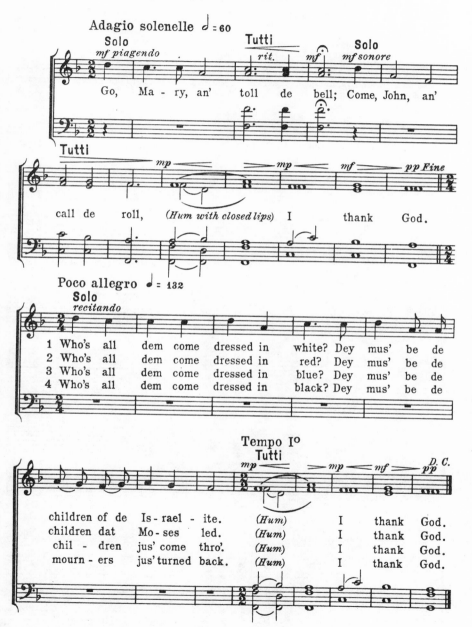

Adagio solenelle ♩=60

Go, Ma-ry, an' toll de bell; Come, John, an' call de roll, (*Hum with closed lips*) I thank God.

Poco allegro ♩=132

1 Who's all dem come dressed in white? Dey mus' be de children of de Is-rael-ite. (*Hum*) I thank God.
2 Who's all dem come dressed in red? Dey mus' be de children dat Mo-ses led. (*Hum*) I thank God.
3 Who's all dem come dressed in blue? Dey mus' be de chil-dren jus' come thro'. (*Hum*) I thank God.
4 Who's all dem come dressed in black? Dey mus' be de mourn-ers jus' turned back. (*Hum*) I thank God.

Tempo I°

Hymns of Judgment
In Dat Great Gittin'-Up Mornin'

This song is a remarkable paraphrase of a portion of the Book of Revelations, and one of the finest specimens of Negro "spirituals." The student who brought it to us and who sings the solo has furnished all that he can remember of the almost interminable succession of verses, which he has heard sung for half an hour at a time by the slaves in their midnight meetings in the woods. He gives the following interesting account of its origin:—

"I have heard my uncle sing this hymn and he told me how it was made. It was made by an old slave who knew nothing about letters or figures. He could not count the number of rails that he would split when he was tasked by his master to split 150 a day. But he tried to lead a Christian life, and he dreamed of the General Judgment, and told his fellow-servants about it, and then made a tune to it and sang it in his cabin meetings." — *J. B. Towe*

156 **Refrain**

f molto con jubilate

In dat great git-tin'-up morn-in' Fare-you-well, Fare - you - well,

sfz ebbollimente

In dat great git-tin'-up morn-in' Fare-you-well, Fare-you-well.

1
2 Dere's a better day a-comin',
3 When my Lord speaks to His Fadder,
4 Says, Fadder, I'm tired o' bearin',
5 Tired o' bearin' for poor sinners,
6 Oh, preachers, fold your Bibles,
7 Prayer-makers, pray no more,
8 For de last soul's converted. *(bis)*

2 *Refrain—*
9 De Lord spoke to Gabriel,
10 Say, go look behind de altar,
11 Take down de silver trumpet,
12 Go down to de seaside,
13 Place one foot on de dry land,
14 Place de oder on de sea,
15 Raise your hand to heaven,
16 Declare by your Maker,
17 Dat time shall be no longer. *(bis)*

3 *Refrain—*
18 Blow your trumpet, Gabriel,
19 Lord, how loud shall I blow it?
20 Blow it right calm and easy,
21 Do not alarm my people,
22 Tell dem to come to judgment. *(bis)*

4 *Refrain—*
23 Den you see de coffins bustin',
24 Den you see de Christians risin',
25 Den you see de righteous marchin',
26 Dey are marchin' home to heaven.
27 Den look upon Mount Zion,
28 You see my Jesus comin',
29 Wid all his holy angels.
30 Where you runnin', sinner?
31 Judgment day is comin'. *(bis)*
Refrain—

5
32 Gabriel, blow your trumpet,
33 Lord, how loud shall I blow it?
34 Loud as seven peals of thunder,
35 Wake de sleepin' nations.
36 Den you see poor sinners risin'.
37 See de dry bones a-creepin',

6 *Refrain—*
38 Den you see de world on fire,
39 You see de moon a-bleedin',
40 See de stars a-fallin'
41 See de elements meltin',
42 See de forked lightnin',
43 Hear de rumblin' thunder.
44 Earth shall reel and totter,
45 Hell shall be uncapped,
46 De dragon shall be loosened.
47 Fare-you-well, poor sinner.

7 *Refrain—*
48 Den you look up in de heaven,
49 See you mother in heaven,
50 While you're doomed to destruction.
51 When de partin' word is given,
52 De Christian shouts to your ruin.
53 No mercy'll ever reach you,

8 *Refrain—*
54 Den you'll cry out for cold water,
55 While de Christian's shoutin' in glory,
56 Sayin' amen to your damnation,
57 Den you hear de sinner sayin',
58 Down I'm rollin', down I'm rollin',
59 Den de righteous housed in heaven,
60 Live wid **God** forever. *(bis)*
Refrain—

My Lord, What a Morning!

Transcribed by the editor from
the singing of the Hampton students
led by Paige I. Lancaster

Largo solenelle *

You'll hear de Christians shout, To wake, etc.
  Look in my God's right hand, When de stars, etc.
You'll hear de angels sing, To wake, etc.
  Look in my God's right hand, When de stars, etc.
Refrain

3

You'll see my Jesus come, To wake, etc.
  Look in my God's right hand, When de stars, etc.
His chariot wheels roll round, To wake, etc.
  Look in my God's right hand, When de stars, etc.
Refrain

* Metronome markings are purposely omitted here, as the pulse, excepting in the solo lines, is neither very pronounced nor regular. — Editor

** The parallel movement of the outside voices, while musically ungrammatical, is nevertheless effective, being not unlike passages in Russian liturgic music. — Editor

Hymns of Judgment
Judgment

Moderato ♩ = 80
marcato

Judg-ment, Judg-ment, Judg-ment Day is a-

roll-in' a-round, Judgment, Judgment, Oh, how I long to go.

Meno mosso ♩ = 60
Solo

I've a good ole mud-der in de heav-en, my Lord,
I've a good ole fad-der in de heav-en, my Lord,

Tutti   **Solo**

Oh, how I long to go dere too; I've a good ole mud-der in de
Oh, how I long to go dere too; I've a good ole fad-der in de

Tutti   **Tempo Iº**

heav-en, my Lord, Oh, how I long to go.
heav-en, my Lord, Oh, how I long to go.   Judg-ment,—

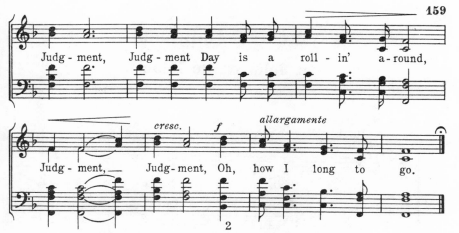

Judg-ment, Judg-ment Day is a roll-in' a-round,

cresc. *f* *allargamente*

Judg-ment,___ Judg-ment, Oh, how I long to go.

2

Dar's a long white robe in de heaven for me,
  Oh, how I long to go dere too;
Dar's a starry crown in de heaven for me,
  Oh, how I long to go.
My name is written in de book ob life,
  Oh, how I long to go dere too,
Ef you look in de book you'll fin' em dar,
  Oh, how I long to go.

3

Brudder Moses gone to de kingdom, Lord,
  Oh, how I long to go dere too;
Sister Mary gone to de kingdom, Lord,
  Oh, how I long to go.
Dar's no more slave in de kingdom, Lord,
  Oh, how I long to go dere too,
All is glory in de kingdom, Lord,
  Oh, how I long to go.

4

My brudder build a house in Paradise,
  Oh, how I long to go dere too;
He built it by dat ribber of life,
  Oh, how I long to go.
Dar's a big camp-meetin' in de kingdom, Lord,
  Oh, how I long to go dere too,
Come, let us jine dat-a heavenly crew,
  Oh, how I long to go.

5

King Jesus sittin' in de kingdom, Lord,
  Oh, how I long to go dere too;
De angles singin' all round de trone,
  Oh, how I long to go.
De trumpet sound de Jubilo,
  Oh, how I long to go dere too,
I hope dat trump will blow me home,
  Oh, how I long to go.

Hymns of Judgment

Put John on de Islan'

Moderato ♩ = 72

Tutti

Hail,— hail,— Put John on de is-lan',

Hail,— hail,— Weep-a low, Judg-ment's com-in'.

Solo — Tutti

1 You got Je-sus, hold Him fas', Weep-a low, Judgment's com in',
2 Didn't know Christ was in-to de fiel', Weep-a low, Judgment's com in',

Solo — Tutti — D. C.

De grace of God you shall re-ceive, Weep-a low, Judgment's comin'.
Till I heard de rumblin' of de char-i-ot wheel, Weep-a low, Judgment's comin'.

3
Gwine down Jordan t' pay my fare,
 Weep-a low, Judgment's comin',
Have a little meetin' when I gits dere,
 Weep-a low, Judgment's comin'.

4
Gwine up t' hebben, don't wan' t' stop,
 Weep-a low, Judgment's comin',
Don't wan' t' be no stumblin' block,
 Weep-a low, Judgment's comin'.

Not a familiar song at Hampton Institute. — Editor

Hymns of Judgment

Oh, the Rocks and the Mountains

2 Doubter, doubter, give up your heart to God,
And you shall have a new hiding-place that day.
Refrain—Oh, the rocks and the mountains, etc.

3 Mourner, mourner, give up your heart to God, etc.

4 Sinner, sinner, give up your heart to God, etc.

5 Sister, sister, give up your heart to God, etc.

6 Mother, mother, give up your heart to God, etc.

7 Children, children, give up your heart to God, etc.

Hymns of Judgment

Stars in the Elements

Moderato devozione ♩ = 88

Refrain
Tutti

O the stars in the el - e-ments are fall - ing, And the moon drips a - way in - to blood, in - to blood, And the ran - somed of the Lord are re - turn - ing home to God. O bless - ed be the name of the Lord!

1 Don't you hear those Chris-tians a - pray - ing, While the moon drips a - way in - to blood, And the in - to blood, ran-somed of the Lord are re - turn - ing home to God? O bless - ed be the name of the Lord!

To Refrain

2
Don't you hear those sinners a-screaming,
While the moon, etc.

3
Don't you hear those sinners a-crying,
While the moon, etc.

Hymns of Judgment

Sweet Turtle Dove, or Jerusalem Mornin'

Solo

mf recitando

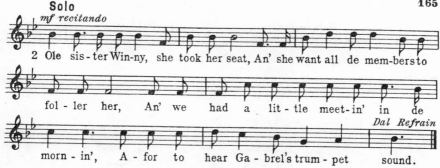

2 Ole sis-ter Win-ny, she took her seat, An' she want all de mem-bers to

fol-ler her, An' we had a lit-tle meet-in' in de

Dal Refrain

morn-in', A-for to hear Ga-brel's trum-pet sound.

3

(Solo)   Ole sister Hannah, she took her seat,
       An' she want all de members to foller her;
    An' we had a little meetin' in de mornin',
       A-for to hear Gabrel's trumpet sound.
    Refrain — Jerusalem mornin', etc.

4

Sweet turtle dove, she sing-a so sweet,
   Muddy de water, so deep,
An' we had a little meetin' in de mornin',
   A-for to hear Gabrel's trumpet sound.
Refrain — Jerusalem mornin', etc.

5

(Solo)   Ole brudder Philip, he took his seat,
       An' he want all de members to foller him;
    An' we had a little meetin' in de mornin',
       A-for to hear Gabrel's trumpet sound.
    Refrain — Jerusalem mornin', etc.

6

(Solo)   Ole sister Hagar, she took her seat,
       An' she want all de members to foller her;
    An' we had a little meetin' in de mornin',
       A-for to hear Gabrel's trumpet sound.
    Refrain — Jerusalem mornin', etc.

7

(Solo)   Ole brudder Moses, he took his seat,
       An' he want all de members to foller him;
    An' we had a little meetin' in de mornin',
       A-for to hear Gabrel's trumpet sound.
    Refrain — Jerusalem mornin', etc.

8

Sweet turtle dove, she sing-a so sweet,
   Muddy de water, so deep,
An' we had a little meetin' in de mornin',
   A-for to hear Gabrel's trumpet sound.
Refrain — Jerusalem mornin', etc.

Hymns of Judgment
When the General Roll Is Called

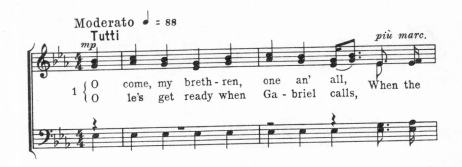

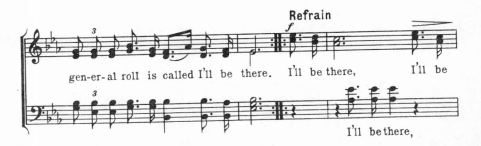

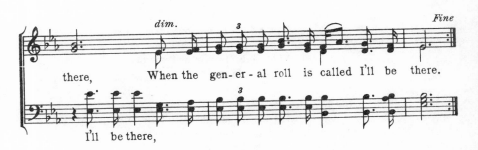

2

Do you belong to the union ban'?
When the general roll is called I'll be there,
Then here's my heart an' here's my han',
When the general roll is called I'll be there.

Hymns of Meditation
Deep River

Andante molto espress.

Deep— river, my home is o-ver Jor-dan,— Deep— river, Lord, I

want to cross o - ver in - to camp-ground, Lord, I

want to cross o - ver in - to camp-ground, Lord, I

want to cross o - ver in - to camp - ground,— Lord, I

want to cross o - ver in - to camp - ground.

1 O don't you want to go to that Gos - pel feast, That

prom - ised land where all is peace? Lord, I

want to cross o - ver in - to camp-ground, Lord, I

want to cross o - ver in - to camp - ground,— Lord, I

want to cross o - ver in - to camp - ground.

2	3
I'll go into heaven and take my seat,	O when I get to heav'n I'll walk all about,
Cast my crown at Jesus' feet.	There's nobody there for to turn me out.

Hymns of Meditation

Dere's a Little Wheel a-Turnin' in My Heart*

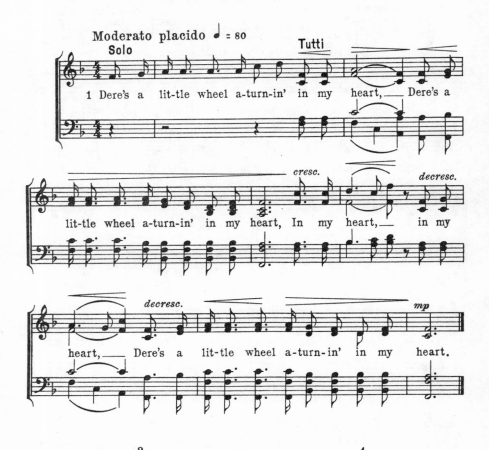

Moderato placido ♩ = 80

1 Dere's a lit-tle wheel a-turn-in' in my heart,— Dere's a lit-tle wheel a-turn-in' in my heart, In my heart,— in my heart,— Dere's a lit-tle wheel a-turn-in' in my heart.

2
‖: O I feel so very happy in my heart, :‖
In my heart, in my heart,
O I feel so very happy in my heart.

3
‖: O I don't feel no ways tired in my heart, :‖
In my heart, in my heart,
O I don't feel no ways tired in my heart.

4
‖: O I feel like shouting in my heart, :‖
In my heart, in my heart,
O I feel like shouting in my heart.

5
‖: I've a double 'termination in my heart, :‖
In my heart, in my heart,
I've a double 'termination in my heart.

*From Tuskegee Collection, by permission

Hymns of Meditation

Ev'ry Time I Feel the Spirit

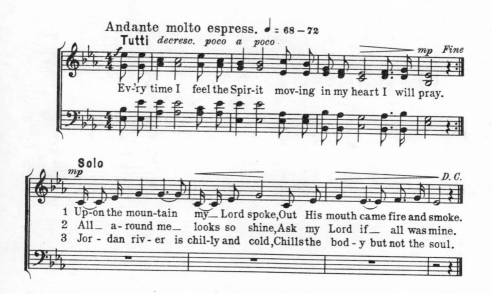

Andante molto espress. ♩ = 68 – 72

Ev-'ry time I feel the Spir-it mov-ing in my heart I will pray.

1 Up-on the moun-tain my— Lord spoke, Out His mouth came fire and smoke.
2 All— a-round me— looks so shine, Ask my Lord if— all was mine.
3 Jor-dan riv-er is chil-ly and cold, Chills the bod-y but not the soul.

Poor Pilgrim

Sung by
Mrs. Eva Evans

Collected by
R. N. D.

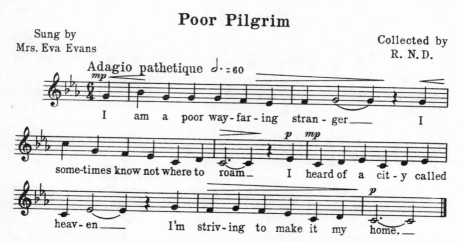

Adagio pathetique ♩. = 60

I am a poor way-far-ing stran-ger— I
some-times know not where to roam— I heard of a cit-y called
heav-en— I'm striv-ing to make it my home.—

Sometimes I'm both tosséd and driven,   My friends and relations forsake me,
I sometimes know not where to roam,   And troubles roll round me so high,
I heard of a city called heaven,   I thought of the kind voice of Jesus
I'm striving to make it my home.   Saying "Poor pilgrim, I'm always nigh."

Hymns of Meditation

I've Been a-List'ning All de Night Long

Allegrezza pianamente ♩ = 92

Refrain
Tutti

mp

I've been a-list-'ning all de night long, Been a-

list-'ning all de day, I've been a-list-'ning all de

poco a poco rit.

night long, To hear some sin-ner pray, pray.

Andante con espressione
Duet

Some say that John de Bap-tist, Was noth-in' but a Jew,

più cresc.

But the Bi-ble doth in-form us Dat he was a preach-er too.

2
Go read the fifth of Matthew,
　An' a-read de chapter thro',
It is a guide to Christians,
　An' a-tells dem what to do.
Refrain—I've been a-list'ning, etc.

3
Dere was a search in heaven,
　An' a-all de earth around,
John stood in sorrow hoping
　Dat a Saviour might be found.
Refrain—I've been a-list'ning, etc.

Hymns of Meditation

Prayer Is de Key of Heaven

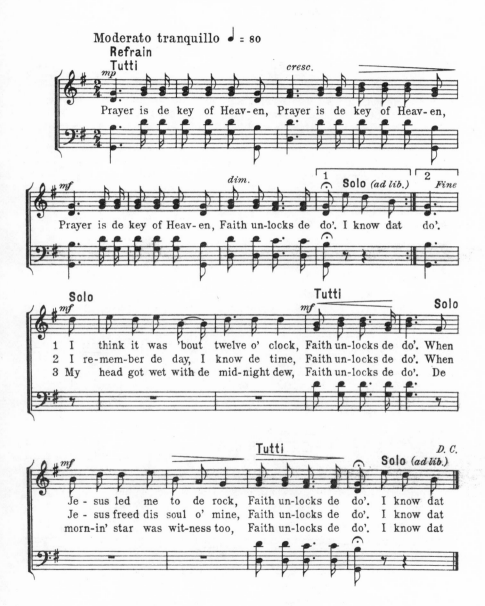

Moderato tranquillo ♩ = 80

Refrain — Tutti

Prayer is de key of Heav-en, Prayer is de key of Heav-en,

Prayer is de key of Heav-en, Faith un-locks de do'. I know dat do'.

Solo (ad lib.)

1. I think it was 'bout twelve o' clock, Faith un-locks de do'. When
2. I re-mem-ber de day, I know de time, Faith un-locks de do'. When
3. My head got wet with de mid-night dew, Faith un-locks de do'. De

Je - sus led me to de rock, Faith un-locks de do'. I know dat
Je - sus freed dis soul o' mine, Faith un-locks de do'. I know dat
morn-in' star was wit-ness too, Faith un-locks de do'. I know dat

Hymns of Meditation

Sometimes I Feel Like a Motherless Child

Lento dolente ♩ = 52

Solo
molto espress. mp

1 Some-times I feel like a moth - er - less child,
2 Ef this was judg - ment day,
3 Some-times I feel like I'm al - mos' gone,

Tutti mf

Some-times I feel like a moth - er - less child,
Ef this was judg - ment day,
Some-times I feel like I'm al - mos' gone,

Some-times I feel like a moth - er - less child,
Ef this was judg - ment day,
Some-times I feel like I'm al - mos' gone,

A long ways from home, A
Eb - 'ry lit - tle soul would pray, Eb
'Way up in de heb - ben - ly lan', 'Way

Solo
mf a piacere

long ways from home. True be - liev - er,
'ry li - tle soul would pray. True be - liev - er,
up in de heb-ben - ly lan'. True be - liev - er,

mp Tutti *decrec.* p pp

A long ways from home, A long ways from home.
Eb - 'ry li - tle soul would pray, Eb - 'ry lit-tle soul would pray.
'Way up in de heb-ben - ly lan', 'Way up in de heb-ben-ly lan'.

Where Shall I Be When de Firs' Trumpet Soun'?

Andante serioso ♩ = 72

Refrain
Tutti

Where shall I be when de firs' trum - pet soun',

cresc

Where shall I be when it soun' so loud, Soun' so loud till it

When it *Fine*

wakes up de dead, Where shall I be when it soun'?

Solo
1 Mos - es__ died in de days of old,
2 God gave de peo - ple de rain - bow sign,

mf recitando

Tutti

Where shall I be?
Where shall I be?

Where he was bur - ied has nev - er been told,
No more wa - ter, but fire__ next time, **Tutti**

Solo
Oh
Oh *D.C.*

Where shall I be?
Where shall I be?

Hymns for Occasions

Bright Sparkles in de Churchyard

This peculiar but beautiful medley was a great favorite among the hands in the tobacco factories in Danville, Va. — *Contributor*

Duo — SOPRANO & TENOR

Bright sparkles in de church-yard, Give light un-to de tomb,

Bright sparkles in de church-yard, Give light un-to de tomb,

Trio — 1st & 2nd SOPRANO & ALTO

Bright sum-mer, spring's o - ver, Sweet flow-ers in dere bloom.

Quartet

Bright sparkles in de church-yard, Give light un-to de tomb, Bright

My moth-er, my

summer, spring's o - ver, Sweet flow-ers in dere bloom. once,

moth-er, In de heav-en, in de

twice, my moth-er, she'll re - joice. once,

heav-en,

twice, In de heav-en she'll re - joice. In de heav-en she'll re - joice.

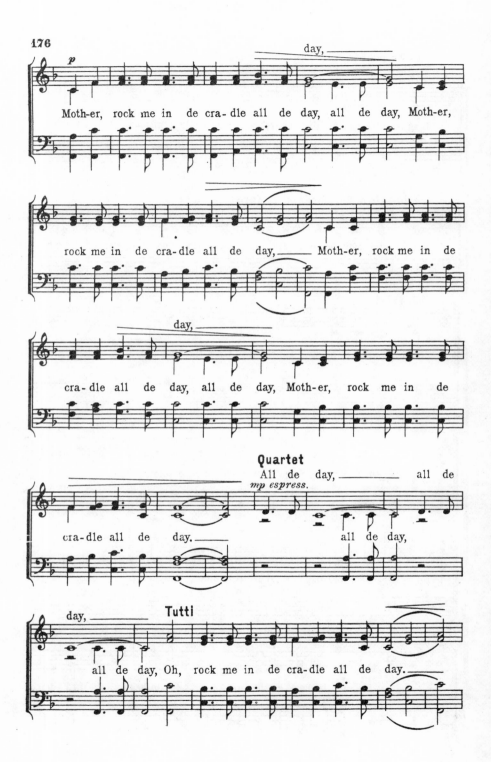

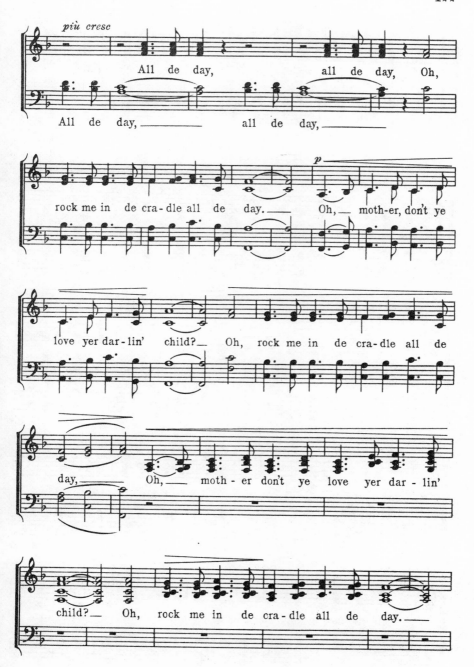

You may lay me down to sleep, my moth-er dear, ___ Oh, rock me in de cra-dle all de day, ___ You may lay me down to sleep, my moth-er dear, ___ Oh, rock me in de cra-dle all de day. ___

Grace Before Meat at Hampton

Harmonized by
R. N. D.

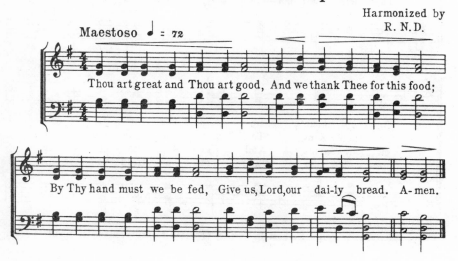

Thou art great and Thou art good, And we thank Thee for this food; By Thy hand must we be fed, Give us, Lord, our dai-ly bread. A-men.

Hymns for Occasions
They Look Like Men of War

While recruiting and drilling the 9th Regiment, U. S. Colored troops at Benedict, Maryland, in the winter of 1863-64, the men gathered around the camp-fire would sing by the hour the melodies of the plantation slave life that they had just left—not always very melodious; but late one evening I was startled by a magnificent chorus from nearly a thousand black soldiers, that called me from my tent to listen to its most inspiring strains, and I caught the following words which I called the "Negro Battle Hymn." — *S. C. Armstrong*

1 Hark! lis - ten to the trum - pet - ers,
2 Their hors - es white, their ar - mor bright,
3 It sets my heart quite in a flame
4 We want no cow - ards in our band,

They call for vol - un - teers; On Zi - on's bright and
With cour - age bold they stand, En - list - ing sol - diers
A sol - dier thus to be; I will en - list, gird
That will their col - ors fly; We call for val - iant -

flow - 'ry mount, Be - hold the of - fi - cers.
for their King To march to Ca - naan's land.
on my arms, And fight for lib - er - ty.
heart - ed men, Who're not a - fraid to die.

The harmonization is by Dr. Herbert B. Turner, Chaplain Emeritus, Hampton Institute — Ed.

5

They follow their great General,
 The great eternal Lamb,
His garment stained in His own blood,
 King Jesus is His name.
Refrain —

6

The trumpets sound, the armies shout,
 They drive the host of hell;
How dreadful is God to adore,
 The great Immanuel!
Refrain —

Hymns for Occasions

There's a Meeting Here To-night

Un poco marziale ♩ = 84

Refrain

Solo — Get you ready, there's a — Tutti — meeting here to-night, Come a-long, there's a — Solo

Tutti — meeting here to-night; I know you by your daily walk, There's a meeting here to-night. *Fine*

Solo — 1 Camp-meet-ing down in the wil-der-ness, There's a meet-ing here to-night; — Tutti — *marcato* — I — Solo

know it's a-mong the Meth-o-dists, There's a — Tutti — meet-ing here to-night. *D. C.*

2

You say you're aiming for the skies,
There's a meeting here to-night;
Why don't you stop your telling lies?
There's a meeting here to-night.

Hymn of Penitence
'Tis Me

Transcribed by the editor from
the singing of the Hampton students
led by Paige I. Lancaster

2 It's not my sister, but it's me, O Lord,

3 It's not my mother, but it's me, O Lord,

4 It's not my elder, but it's me, O Lord,

* The tendency toward improvisation on the part of certain groups of the chorus is illustrated also in Ole-Time Religion p. 200, and I Couldn't Hear Nobody Pray, p. 202. — Editor

Hymns of Pilgrimage
A Wheel in a Wheel

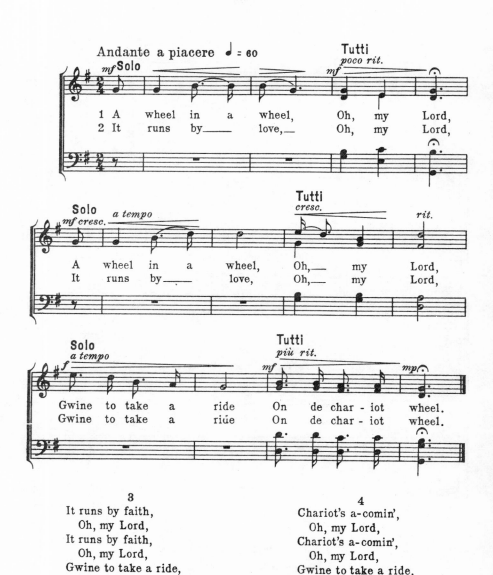

1 A wheel in a wheel, Oh, my Lord,
2 It runs by love, Oh, my Lord,

A wheel in a wheel, Oh, my Lord,
It runs by love, Oh, my Lord,

Gwine to take a ride On de char - iot wheel.
Gwine to take a ride On de char - iot wheel.

3
It runs by faith,
Oh, my Lord,
It runs by faith,
Oh, my Lord,
Gwine to take a ride,
On de chariot wheel.

4
Chariot's a-comin',
Oh, my Lord,
Chariot's a-comin',
Oh, my Lord,
Gwine to take a ride,
On de chariot wheel.

Hymns of Pilgrimage

Hail! Hail! Hail!

Giocoso ♩ = 88

Refrain

Children, hail! hail! hail! I'm gwine jine saints a-bove;

Hail! hail! hail! I'm on my jour-ney home. *Fine*

Solo — O look up yan-der, what I see, I'm on my jour-ney home; Chorus

Solo — Bright an-gels com-in' ar-ter me, I'm on my jour-ney home. Chorus *D. C.*

2
If you git dere before I do,
 I'm on my journey home,
Look out for me,—I'm comin' too;
 I'm on my journey home.
Refrain—Children, hail, etc.

3
Oh, hallelujah to de Lamb!
 I'm on my journey home,
King Jesus died for ebry man,
 I'm on my journey home.
Refrain—Children, hail, etc.

Hymns of Pilgrimage

I'm a-Rolling*

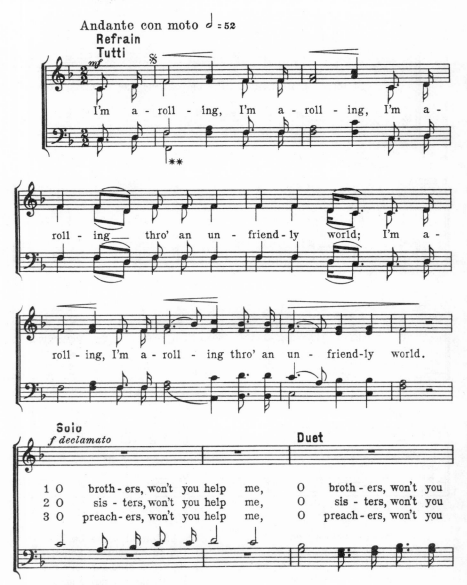

Andante con moto ♩=52

Refrain
Tutti

I'm a - roll - ing, I'm a - roll - ing, I'm a-
roll - ing___ thro' an un - friend-ly world; I'm a-
roll - ing, I'm a - roll - ing thro' an un - friend-ly world.

Solo
f declamato

Duet

1 O broth - ers, won't you help me, O broth - ers, won't you
2 O sis - ters, won't you help me, O sis - ters, won't you
3 O preach- ers, won't you help me, O preach- ers, won't you

* Fisk Jubilee Collection, by permission
** Lower octave used after D. S.

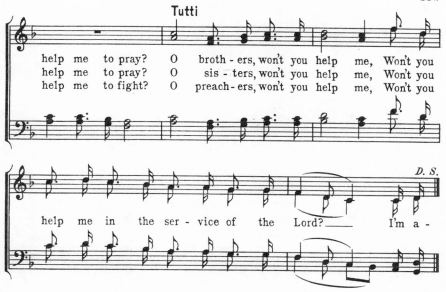

help me to pray? O broth-ers, won't you help me, Won't you
help me to pray? O sis - ters, won't you help me, Won't you
help me to fight? O preach-ers, won't you help me, Won't you

help me in the ser - vice of the Lord?___ I'm a -

I'm a-Trav'ling to the Grave *

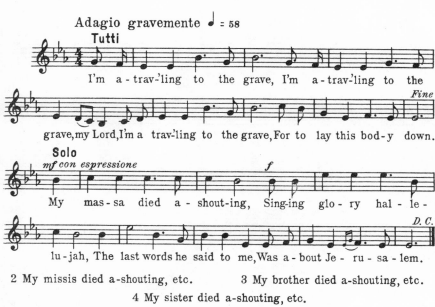

Adagio gravemente ♩ = 58

Tutti

I'm a - trav-'ling to the grave, I'm a - trav-'ling to the

grave, my Lord, I'm a trav-'ling to the grave, For to lay this bod-y down.

Solo
mf con espressione   *f*

My mas-sa died a - shout-ing, Sing-ing glo - ry hal - le -

lu - jah, The last words he said to me, Was a - bout Je - ru - sa - lem.

2 My missis died a-shouting, etc.   3 My brother died a-shouting, etc.

4 My sister died a-shouting, etc.

*Fisk Jubilee Collection, by permission

Hymns of Pilgrimage
Sweet Canaan

My mother used to tell me how the colored people all expected to be free some day, and how one night a great many of them met together in a cabin, and tied little budgets on their backs as though they expected to go off somewhere, and cried, and shook hands, and sang this hymn.

— *Alice Davis*

Moderato giusto ♩ = 80

mf Tutti

Oh, de land I am bound for, Sweet Ca-naan's hap-py land I am

bound for, Sweet Ca-naan's hap-py land I am bound for, Sweet

Ca-naan's hap-py land, Pray give me your right hand, hand.

mp   *mf* Tutti

Oh, my broth-er, did you come for to help me,
Oh, my sis-ter, did you come for to help me,

cresc.

Oh, my broth-er, did you come for to help me, Oh, my broth-er, did you
Oh, my sis-ter, did you come for to help me, Oh, my sis-ter, did you

mp

come for to help me? Pray, give me your right hand,
come for to help me? Pray, give me   your right hand.

Hymns of Pilgrimage

Oh, Stand the Storm

Con anima ♩ = 80

Refrain

Oh, stand the storm, it won't be long, We'll an-chor by and by;

Stand the storm, it won't be long, We'll an-chor by___ and by.

1 My ship is on___ the o-cean, We'll an-chor by and by; My

ship is on___ the o-cean, We'll an-chor by___ and by.

D. C. Refrain

2
She's making for the kingdom,
  We'll anchor by and by:
She's making for the king lom,
  We'll anchor by and by.

3
I've a mother in the kingdom,
  We'll anchor by and by;
I've a mother in the kingdom,
  We'll anchor by and by.

4
We're crossing over Jordan,
  We'll anchor by and by;
We're crossing over Jordan,
  We'll anchor by and by.

5
King Jesus is our captain,
  We'll anchor by and by;
King Jesus is our captain,
  We'll anchor by and by.

Hymns of Pilgrimage

Oh, Jerusalem!

Moderato assai ♩ = 72

Tutti

Oh, Je - ru - sa - lem! Oh, my Lord! I'm walk - in' de road,

Oh, Je - ru - sa - lem, walk - in' de road   Oh, my Lord!   Oh, my Lord!

Solo
poco più moto

1 Mind, my sis - ter, how you walk on de cross, Yo'
2 My Lord God A' might - y come step - pin' down, Come
3 Sea of glass all min - gled wid fire, Good -

foot might slip an' yo' soul git los'!
step - pin' down on a sea of glass!
bye, my brud - der, I'm goin' on higher!

This must be a very old, or very obscure song as I have been unable to find anyone who knows it. The markings therefore are merely suggestive of its probably best interpretation. — Editor

Hymns of Pilgrimage
Pilgrim's Song

Moderato espressivo ♩ = 72

Tutti

mp

1 I'm a poor way - far - in' strang-er, While jour - ney -
2 I know dark clouds will gath-er round me, I know my
3 I'll soon be free from ev - 'ry trial, My bod - y

in' thro' this world of woe, Yet there's no sick - ness, toil, and
way— is rough an' steep, Yet bright fields lie just be -
will sleep in the ole church - yard, I'll drop the cross of self - de -

mf

dan - ger, In that bright world to which I go. I'm go - in'
fore me, Where God's re - deemed their vi - gils keep. I'm go - in'
ni - al, An' en - ter on— my great re - ward. I'm go - in'

there— to see my fa - ther, I'm go - in' there no more to roam,
there— to see my moth er, She said she'd meet me when I come,
there— to see my Sav - iour, To sing His praise in heav-en's dome,

dim. poco a poco

2d time *pp*

I'm just a - go - in' o - ver Jor - dan, I'm just a - go - in' o - ver home.

Bass (hum 2d time)

Hymns of Pilgrimage

Roll de Ole Chariot Along

Tempo di marcia ♩ = 116

Oh, roll de ole__ char-iot a-long, Roll de ole__ char-iot a-long,

Roll de ole__ char-iot a-long, Ef ye don't hang on be-hin'.

Solo

1 We are trav-el-lin' from man-sions to man-sions, to man-sions,

We are trav-el-lin' from man-sions to man-sions, to man-sions,

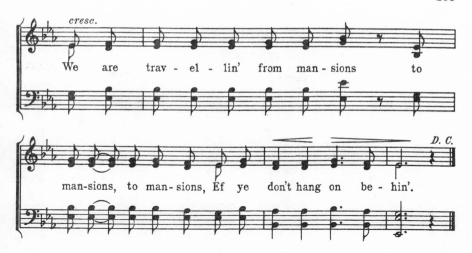

We are trav-el-lin' from man-sions to man-sions, to man-sions, Ef ye don't hang on be-hin'.

2

‖: Gwine t'jine wid de hundred
    An' forty-fo' thousand, :‖
    Ef ye don't hang on behin'.

3

‖: Ef my farder will go
    He shall wear a starry crown, :‖
    Ef ye don't hang on behin'.

4

‖: Ef my mudder will go
    She shall wear a starry crown, :‖
    Ef ye don't hang on behin'.

5

‖: Ef de elder will go
    He shall wear a starry crown, :‖
    Ef ye don't hang on behin'.

6

‖: Ef de preacher's in de way,
    Jus' roll him over, :‖
    Ef ye don't hang on behin'.

7

‖: Ef de deacon will go
    He shall wear a starry crown, :‖
    Ef ye don't hang on behin'.

Hymns of Praise
Ride On

Moderato con moto ♩ = 80

Refrain
Tutti

Ride___ on, ride__ on, Ride on, King E- man-u - el..

Don't you wan' t' go t' heb-ben in de morn in'?

Solo
f declamato   *mf* Tutti

1 Some of dese morn - in's bright an' fair,___ Don't you
2 Some of dese morn - in's bright an' fair,___ Don't you
3 You say you're aim - in' for de skies,___ Don't you

Solo

wan' t' go t' heb-ben in de morn-in'? Take my flight up to de skies,
wan' t' go t' heb-ben in de morn-in'? Take my flight right thro' de air,___
wan' t' go t' heb-ben in de morn-in'? Why don't you stop tell - in' lies,

Tutti   D. C.

Don't you wan' t' go t' heb - ben in de morn in'?

Hymns of Praise

Let Us Praise Him

Moderato con devozione ♩ = 72
Tutti

1 Let us praise_ Him, Let us praise_ Him,
2 I_ once was los' But now I am foun',
3 I_ nev - er shall for - get dat day,

Glo - ry, Hal - le - lu - jah!_ Let us praise_ Him,
Glo - ry, Hal - le - lu - jah!_ I_ once was los'
Glo - ry, Hal - le - lu - jah!_ When Je - sus wash'

O _ praise, O praise, Glo - ry, Hal - le - lu - jah!
But now I am foun', Glo - ry, Hal - le - lu - jah!
my_ sins a - way, Glo - ry, Hal - le - lu - jah!

4
'Twas little I thought He was so nigh,
Glory, Hallelujah!
He spoke and He made me laugh and cry,—
Glory, Hallelujah!

Verse 4 supplied by Dr. Robert R. Moton, Principal Tuskegee Institute, Ala.

Hymns of Praise
Zion, Weep a-Low

Solo
Say, what sort o' sword dat you talk-in' 'bout? Den-a
cresc.

Tutti
decisivo
Hal - le - lu - jah to-a de Lamb,

Solo
mp
I'm talk-in' 'bout dat

two-edged sword, Den-a

Tutti
decisivo
mp
Hal - le - lu - jah to-a de Lamb.

Solo
Oh
D.C.

2
Oh, look up yonder, Lord, a-what I see,
  Den-a Hallelujah, etc.
Dere's a long tall angel a-comin' a'ter me,
  Den-a Hallelujah, etc.
Wid a palms o' vicatry in-a my hand,
  Den-a Hallelujah, etc.
Wid a golden crown a-placed on-a my head,
  Den-a Hallelujah, etc.
Chorus — Oh, Zion, weep-a low.

3
Zion been a-weepin' all o' de day,
  Den-a Hallelujah, etc.
Say, come, poor sinners, come-a an' pray,
  Den-a Hallelujah, etc.
Oh, Satan, like-a dat huntin' dog,
  Den-a Hallelujah, etc.
He hunt dem-a Christians home to God,
  Den-a Hallelujah, etc.
Chorus — Oh, Zion, weep-a low.

4
Oh, hebben so high, an' I so low,
  Den-a Hallelujah, etc.
I don' know shall I ebber get to hebben or no,
  Den-a Hallelujah, etc.
Gwine to tell my brudder befo' I go,
  Den-a Hallelujah, etc.
What a dolesome road-a I had to go,
  Den-a Hallelujah, etc.
Chorus — Oh, Zion, weep-a low.

Hymns of Praise

Rise an' Shine

♩ = 96
Refrain
Tutti f

Oh,__ rise an' shine, an' give God de glo-ry, glo-ry, Rise an'

cresc.

Rise an' shine, an'

shine, an' give God de glo-ry, glo-ry, Rise an' shine, an'

Rise shine

give God de glo-ry, glo-ry, For de year of Ju-ber-lee.

Je - sus car - ry de young lambs
Je - sus lead de ole sheep

Je - sus car - ry de young lambs in his bo - som, bo - som,
Je - sus lead__ de ole sheep by still wa - ters, wa - ters,

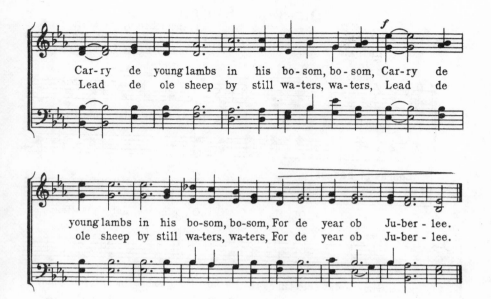

Car-ry de young lambs in his bo-som, bo-som, Car-ry de
Lead de ole sheep by still wa-ters, wa-ters, Lead de

young lambs in his bo-som, bo-som, For de year ob Ju-ber-lee.
ole sheep by still wa-ters, wa-ters, For de year ob Ju-ber-lee.

2

Oh, come on, mourners, get you ready, ready,
Come on, mourners, get you ready, ready,
Come on, mourners, get you ready, ready,
    For de year ob Juberlee;
You may keep your lamps trimmed an' burning, burning,
Keep your lamps trimmed an' burning, burning,
Keep your lamps trimmed an' burning, burning,
    For de year ob Juberlee.
Refrain—Oh, rise an' shine, etc.

3

Oh, come on, children, don't be weary, weary,
Come on, children, don't be weary, weary,
Come on, children, don't be weary, weary,
    For de year ob Juberlee;
Oh, don't you hear dem bells a-ringin', ringin',
Don't you hear dem bells a-ringin', ringin',
Don't you hear dem bells a-ringin', ringin',
    For de year ob Juberlee?
Refrain—Oh, rise an' shine, etc.

Hymns of Religion

Ole-Time Religion

Transcribed by the editor from
the singing of the Hampton students
led by Paige I. Lancaster

♩ = 76

Refrain

Solo molto ritmo — *Tutti* — *Solo*

Gim me dat ole-time re - lig-ion, Gim me dat ole-time re-

Chorus of basses *f > sf*

Ole-time, O gim me dat ole-time

cresc.

lig-ion, Gim me dat ole-time re - lig-ion, It's good e - nough for me.

O gim me dat ole-time re - lig-ion, It's good e - nough for me.

Solo — *Tutti cresc.*

It was good for my ole fa - ther, It was good for my ole

cresc. — *D. C.*

fa-ther, It was good for my ole fa-ther, It's good e - nough for me.

2 It was good for my ole mother,—
3 It was good for Paul and Silas,—
4 Makes me love ev'rybody,—

5 It is good when I'm in trouble,—
6 It will do when I am dying,—
7 It will take us all to heaven,—

The striking extra chorus of basses is a good example of the tendency toward improvization on the part of the students.—Editor

Hymns of Religion
Oh, Religion Is a Fortune

2

Gwine to sit down in de kingdom, I raly do believe, Whar sabbaths have, etc.
Gwine to walk about in Zion, I raly do believe, Whar sabbaths have, etc.
Duet — Whar ye been, young convert, etc. — *Refrain*

3

Gwine to see my sister Mary, I raly do believe, Whar sabbaths have, etc.
Gwine to see my brudder Jonah, I raly do believe, Whar sabbaths have, etc.
Duet — Whar ye been, good Christian, etc. — *Refrain*

4

Gwine to talk-a wid de angels, I raly do believe, Whar sabbaths have, etc.
Gwine to see my massa Jesus, I raly do believe, Whar sabbaths have, etc.

*Repeat music from here to Fine for verses 2, 3, and 4 — Editor

— *Refrain*

Hymns of Religious Experience

I Couldn't Hear Nobody Pray

Transcribed by
R. Nathaniel Dett

*This extra chorus of tenors is a small group, usually with striking voices who sing in a rather improvisatory way. See also the footnote to 'Tis Me, p. 183 and to Ole-Time Religion, p. 200 — Editor

2

Solo
Chilly waters!
Chorus
I couldn't hear nobody pray,
Solo
In the Jordan!
Chorus
I couldn't hear nobody pray,
Solo
Crossing over!
Chorus
I couldn't hear nobody pray,
Solo
Into Canaan!
Chorus
I couldn't hear nobody pray,
Solo
O Lord!
Refrain

3

Solo
Hallelujah!
Chorus
I couldn't hear nobody pray,
Solo
Troubles over!
Chorus
I couldn't hear nobody pray,
Solo
In the kingdom!
Chorus
I couldn't hear nobody pray,
Solo
With my Jesus!
Chorus
I couldn't hear nobody pray,
Solo
O Lord!
Refrain

Hymns of Religious Experience
I Heard From Heaven To-day

"A secret prayer-meeting song, sung by Thomas Vess, a blacksmith and a slave. He especially sang it when any one confessed religion. Thomas Vess was a man whose heart was given to these songs, for in the neighborhood where he lived, it seemed like a prayer-meeting did not go on well without him. I have long since learned wherever he was known what happiness he got from them."
— *J. M. Waddy*

1 Oh, Pe-ter, go ring dem bells, Pe-ter, go_ ring dem bells, Pe-ter, go ring dem bells, I heard from heav-en to - day.

Solo
I won-der where my *Al Chorus after D.C.* moth-er is gone, **Chorus**

I won-der where my_ moth-er is gone, I won-der where my_ moth-er is gone, I heard from heav-en to - day.

I heard from heav-en to-day, I heard from heav-en to-day, I thank God, and I thank you too, I heard from heav-en to-day.

2

I wonder where sister Mary's gone —
I heard from heaven to-day;
I wonder where sister Martha's gone —
I heard from heaven to-day;
It's good news, and I thank God —
I heard from heaven to-day;
Oh, Peter, go ring dem bells —
I heard from heaven to-day.
Chorus—I heard from heaven, etc.

3

I wonder where brudder Moses' gone —
I heard from heaven to-day;
I wonder where brudder Daniel's gone —
I heard from heaven to-day;
He's gone where Elijah has gone —
I heard from heaven to-day;
Oh, Peter, go ring dem bells —
I heard from heaven to-day.
Chorus—I heard from heaven, etc.

Hymns of Religious Experience

Hear de Angels Singin'

Moderato piacevale ♩ = 80
Refrain
Tutti

Oh, sing all de way,— sing all— de way,—

Sing all de way, my Lord, Hear de an-gels sing-in'.

mf Solo

We're march-in up to heb-ben, it's a hap-py time;
An' Je - sus is on - a de— mid-dle line;
Dem-a Chris - tians take up— too much time;
Dey're i - dlin' on— dat bat-tle line;

Hear de an-gels sing-in'.

2

Now all things well, an' I don't dread hell;
Hear de angels singin',
I am goin' up to hebben, where my Jesus dwell;
Hear de angels singin',
For de angels are callin' me away,
Hear de angels singin',
An' I must go, I cannot stay,
Hear de angels singin'.
Chorus—Oh, sing, etc.

3

Now take your Bible, an' read it through;
Hear de angels singin',
An' ebery word you'll find is true;
Hear de angels singin',
For in dat Bible you will see,
Hear de angels singin',
Dat Jesus died for you an' me,
Hear de angels singin'.
Chorus—Oh, sing, etc.

4

Say, if my memory sarves me right,
Hear de angels singin',
We're sure to hab a little shout tonight,
Hear de angels singin',
For I love to shout, I love to sing,
Hear de angels singin',
I love to praise my Hebbenly King,
Hear de angels singin'.
Chorus—Oh, sing, etc.

Hymns of Religious Experience

I Know the Lord's Laid His Hands on Me

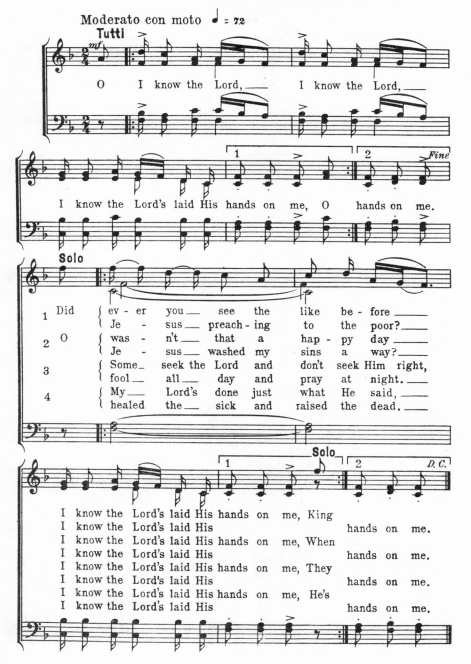

Hymns of Religious Experience
Leanin' on de Lord

"My father sang this hymn, and said he knew a time when a great many slaves were allowed to have a revival for two days, while their masters and their families had one; and a great many professed religion. And one poor, ignorant man professed religion, and praised God, and sang this hymn."
— *A Hampton Student*

Oh, broth-er, how d'ye
I felt__ so__

wil-der-ness, come out de wil-der-ness.
wil-der-ness, come out de wil-der-ness.

feel__
hap-py__

Chorus

when ye come out de wil-der-ness, Lean-in' on de Lord.
when I come out de wil-der-ness, Lean-in' on de Lord.

Refrain

Oh, lean-in' on de Lord,__ Lean-in' on de Lord, Oh,

lean-in' up-on de Lamb of God, who was slain on Cal-va-ry.

2

I shouted Hallelujah, when I, etc.
   Leanin' on de Lord;
I heard de angels singin', when I, etc.
   Leanin' on de Lord;
I heard de harps a harpin' when I, etc.
   Leanin' on de Lord.

Refrain — Oh, leanin' on de Lord.

3

I heard de angels moanin', when I, etc.
   Leanin' on de Lord;
I heard de deb'l howlin', when I, etc.
   Leanin' on de Lord;
I gib de deb'l a battle, when I, etc.
   Leanin' on de Lord.

Refrain — Oh, leanin' on de Lord.

Hymns of Religious Experience

Oh, Yes!

Moderato con moto ♩ = 92

Chorus repeats these two measures ✱ *mf*

Solo: I tell ye, breth-er-en, a mor-tal fac',—

Oh, yes! Oh, yes!

Tutti — Solo: Ef ye want to get to heav'n, don't nebber look back,

Oh, yes! Oh, yes!

Tutti — Solo: I want to know-a be-fore I go,— Tutti

Oh, yes! Oh, yes! — Oh, yes! Oh, yes!

Solo: Yea, wheth-er you love-a de Lord or no,— Tutti

Oh, yes! Oh, yes!

✱ But not always.

2

If ebber I land on de oder sho', Oh, yes, Oh, yes!
I'll nebber come here for to sing no mo', Oh, yes, Oh, yes!
A golden band all round my waist, Oh, yes, Oh, yes!
An' de palms ob vic-a-try in-a my hand, Oh, yes, Oh, yes!
An' de golden slippers on to my feet, Oh, yes, Oh, yes!
Gwine to walk up an' down o' dem golden street. Oh, yes, Oh, yes!
Refrain-Oh, wait till I put on my robe.

3

An' my lovely bretheren, dat aint all, Oh, yes, Oh, yes!
I'm not done a talkin' about my Lord; Oh, yes, Oh, yes!
An' a golden crown a-placed on-a my head, Oh, yes, Oh, yes!
An' my long white robe a-come a-dazzlin' down, Oh, yes, Oh, yes!
Now wait till I get on my gospel shoes, Oh, yes, Oh, yes!
Gwine to walk about de heaben an' a-carry de news. Oh, yes, Oh, yes!
Refrain-Oh, wait till I put on my robe.

4

I'm anchored in Christ, Christ anchored in me, Oh, yes, Oh, yes!
All de deb'ls in hell can't-a-pluck a-me out, Oh, yes, Oh, yes!
An' I wonder what Satan's grumbulin' about, Oh, yes, Oh, yes!
He's bound into hell, an' he can't git out, Oh, yes, Oh, yes!
But he shall be loose an' hab his sway, Oh, yes, Oh, yes!
Yea at de great resurrection day. Oh, yes, Oh, yes!
Refrain-Oh, wait till I put on my robe.

Verses, some of which are often added

5

I went down de hill side to make-a one prayer, Oh, yes, Oh, yes!
An' when I got dere, old Satan was dere, Oh, yes, Oh, yes!
An' what do ye t'ink he said to me? Oh, yes, Oh, yes!
Said, "Off from here you'd better be," Oh, yes, Oh, yes!
An' what for to do, I did not know, Oh, yes, Oh, yes!
But I fell on my knees, an' I cried, Oh, yes, Oh, yes!
Now my Jesus bein' so good an' kind, Oh, yes, Oh, yes!
Yea, to de with-er-ed, halt, an' blind; Oh, yes, Oh, yes!
My Jesus lowered his mercy down. Oh, yes, Oh, yes!
An' snatch-a-me from dem doors ob hell, Oh, yes, Oh, yes!
He snatch-a-me from dem doors ob hell, Oh, yes, Oh, yes!
An' took-a me in-a wid him to dwell. Oh, yes, Oh, yes!
Refrain-Oh, wait till I put on my robe.

6

I was in de church an' prayin' loud, Oh, yes, Oh, yes!
An' on my knees to my Jesus bowed, Oh, yes, Oh, yes!
Ole Satan tole me to my face, Oh, yes, Oh, yes!
"I'll git you when-a you leave dis place;" Oh, yes, Oh, yes!
Oh, brother, dat scare me to my heart, Oh, yes, Oh, yes!
I was 'fraid to walk-a when it was dark. Oh, yes, Oh, yes!
Refrain-Oh, wait till I put on my robe.

7

I started home, but I did pray, Oh, yes, Oh, yes!
An' I met ole Satan on de way; Oh, yes, Oh, yes!
Ole Satan made-a one grab at me. Oh, yes, Oh, yes!
But he missed my soul, an' I went free. Oh, yes, Oh, yes!
My sins went a-lumberin' down to hell, Oh, yes, Oh, yes!
An' my soul went a-leapin' up Zion's hill; Oh, yes, Oh, yes!
I tell ye what, bretherin, you'd better not laugh, Oh, yes, Oh, yes!
Ole Satan'll run you down his path; Oh, yes, Oh, yes!
If he runs you, as he run me, Oh, yes, Oh, yes!
You'll be glad to fall upon your knee. Oh, yes, Oh, yes!
Refrain-Oh, wait till I put on my robe.

Hymn of the Resurrection

Dust an' Ashes

Andante un poco pesante ♩= 72

Tutti

1 Dust, dust an' ash-es fly o-ver on my grave,

Dust, dust an' ash-es fly o-ver on my grave, Dust, dust an'

ash-es fly o-ver on my grave, An' de Lord shall bear my

quasi echo
semi chorus (ad lib.)

spir - it home, An' de Lord shall bear my spir - it home.

The expression marks indicate the interpretation of this famous song as given at the church service each Easter Sunday at Hampton Institute, under the direction of the editor.

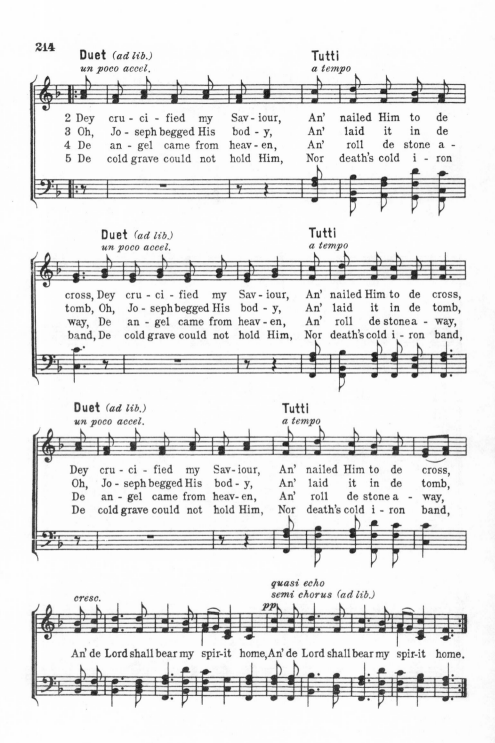

Duet *(ad lib.)* — *un poco accel.* — **Tutti** — *a tempo*

2 Dey cru-ci-fied my Sav-iour, An' nailed Him to de cross, Dey cru-ci-fied my Sav-iour, An' nailed Him to de cross,

3 Oh, Jo-seph begged His bod-y, An' laid it in de tomb, Oh, Jo-seph begged His bod-y, An' laid it in de tomb,

4 De an-gel came from heav-en, An' roll de stone a-way, De an-gel came from heav-en, An' roll de stone a-way,

5 De cold grave could not hold Him, Nor death's cold i-ron band, De cold grave could not hold Him, Nor death's cold i-ron band,

Dey cru-ci-fied my Sav-iour, An' nailed Him to de cross,
Oh, Jo-seph begged His bod-y, An' laid it in de tomb,
De an-gel came from heav-en, An' roll de stone a-way,
De cold grave could not hold Him, Nor death's cold i-ron band,

cresc. — *quasi echo* — *semi chorus (ad lib.)* — *pp*

An' de Lord shall bear my spir-it home, An' de Lord shall bear my spir-it home.

Allegro jiocoso
Refrain
Tutti

He rose, He rose, He rose from de dead,

He rose, He rose,

He rose, He rose, He rose from de dead,

He rose, He rose,

He rose, He rose, He rose from de dead, An' de

He rose, He rose,

rit. forte et molto allargamente

Lord shall bear my spir-it home, An' de Lord shall bear my spir-it home.

Tempo I

Duet (*ad lib.*) **Tutti**
un poco accel. *a tempo*

6 Oh, Ma - ry came a - run - nin', Her Sav - iour for to

Duet (*ad lib.*) **Tutti**
un poco accel. *a tempo*

see, Oh, Ma - ry came a - run - nin', Her Sav - iour for to see,

Duet (*ad lib.*) **Tutti**
un poco accel. *a tempo*

Oh, Ma - ry came a - run - nin', Her Sav - iour for to see, —

cresc. *quasi echo*
semi chorus (ad lib.)
pp

An' de Lord shall bear my spir-it home, An' de Lord shall bear my spir-it home.

piacevole *più marcato*
mp

7 De an - gel say He is not here, He's gone to Gal - i - lee, De
poco

an - gel say He is not here, He's gone to Gal - i - lee, De

cresc.

an-gel say He is not here, He's gone to＿ Gal-i-lee. An' de Lord shall

più allargamente

bear my spir-it home, An' de Lord＿ shall bear＿ my spir-it＿ home.

Al rigore di tempo
Tutti

De an-gel say He is not here, He's gone to Gal-i-lee.

De an-gel say He is not here, He's gone to Gal-i-lee.

cresc.   *sf*   *sf*   *sf*   *sf*   *sf*   *sf*   *sf*

De an-gel say He is not here, He's gone to Gal-i-lee.

cresc.   *f*

An' de Lord shall bear my spir-it home,

Hymns of the Second Coming
Oh, Yes, Yonder Comes My Lord

Allegretto ♩ = 116

Tutti

1 Oh, yes, yon - der comes my Lord,—

Oh, yes, yon - der comes my Lord,—

Oh, yes, yon - der comes my Lord,

Oh, yes, yon - der comes my Lord, Oh, yes, yon - der comes my Lord,

Oh, yes, yon - der comes my Lord,

Oh, yes, yon - der comes my Lord,

Oh, yes, yon - der comes my Lord, Oh, yes, yon - der comes my,

Oh, yes, yon - der comes my,

Oh, yes, yon - der comes my, Oh, yes, yon - der comes my Lord.

2 He is comin' this-a way.

3 With His sword in His han'.

4 He's gwine t'hew dem sinners down.

5 Right level to de groun.

Not a familiar song at Hampton Institute. — Editor

Hymns of the Second Coming

Don't You View Dat Ship a-Come a-Sailin?

Solo

For 2d and all succeeding verses

tranquillo

Dat ship is heav-y load-ed, Hal-le - lu - jah,

Dat___ ship is heav - y___ load - ed, Dat___

ship is heav - y___ load - ed, Dat___

ship is heav - y___ load - ed Hal - le - lu - jah.

2 Dat ship is heavy loaded, Hallelujah.

3 She neither reels nor totters, Hallelujah.

4 She is loaded wid-a bright angels, Hallelujah.

5 Oh, how do you know dey are angels? Hallelujah.

6 I know dem by a de'r mournin', Hallelujah.

7 Oh, yonder comes my Jesus, Hallelujah.

8 Oh, how do you know it is Jesus? Hallelujah.

9 I know him by-a his shinin', Hallelujah.

Hymns of Tribulation

Hard Trials

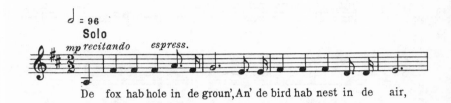

De fox hab hole in de groun', An' de bird hab nest in de air,

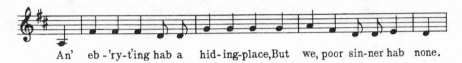

An' eb-'ry-t'ing hab a hid-ing-place, But we, poor sin-ner hab none.

Refrain
Tutti

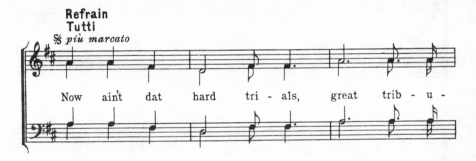

Now ain't dat hard tri - als, great trib - u -

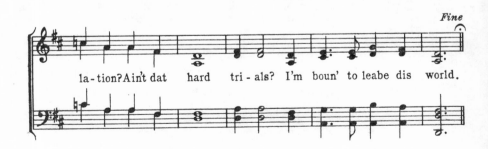

la - tion? Ain't dat hard tri - als? I'm boun' to leabe dis world.

Solo

1 Bap - tist, Bap - tist is my name, Bap - tist till I die, I'll
2 Meth-o-dist, Meth-o-dist is my name, Meth-o-dist till I die, I'll
3 Presbyterian, Presbyterian is my name, Presbyterian till I die, I'll

D. S. Refrain al Fine

be bap-tize in de Bap - tist name, An' I'll lib on de Bap - tist side.
be bap-tize in de Meth-o-dist name, An' I'll lib on de Meth-o-dist side.
be bap-tize in de Presbyterian name, An' I'll lib on de Presbyterian side.

4 You may go dis - a way, You may go dat - a way, You may

go from do' to do', But ef you hab-n't got de grace ob

D. S. Refrain al Fine

God in you heart, De deb - il will get you sho'.

marcato e poco meno mosso

5 Now while we are march-in' a - long dis dread-ful road, You had

D. S. Refrain al Fine

bet-ter stop your dif-fer-ent names, An' take up de heb-ben-ly load.

In this song it is very effective to have each verse sung by a different solo voice as if the various contributions to the discussion were made by different individuals, as they probably were originally.

Hymns of Tribulation

Hear de Lambs a-Cryin'

2

I don' know what you want to stay here for, Oh, shepherd, etc.
For dis vain world's no friend to grace, Oh, shepherd, etc.
If I only had wings like Noah's dove, Oh, shepherd, etc.
I'd fly away to de heavens above, Oh, shepherd, etc.
Refrain—You hear de lambs a-cryin', etc.

3

When I am in an agony, Oh, shepherd, etc.
When you see me, pity me, Oh, shepherd, etc.
For I am a pilgrim travellin' on, Oh, shepherd, etc.
De lonesome road where Jesus gone, Oh, shepherd, etc.
Refrain—You hear de lambs a-cryin', etc.

4

Oh, see my Jesus hanging high, Oh, shepherd, etc.
He looked so pale an' bled so free, Oh, shepherd, etc.
Oh, don't you think it was a shame, Oh, shepherd, etc.
He hung three hours in dreadful pain? Oh, shepherd, etc.
Refrain—You hear de lambs a-cryin', etc.

Hymns of Tribulation

I've Been Toilin' at de Hill

1 Oh, moth-er, ain't you glad? Moth-er,— ain't you
2 Oh, fa-ther, ain't you glad? fa-ther, ain't you

Oh, yes,
basso molto devozione

molto cresc.   *f*

glad? Oh, moth-er, ain't you glad, my Lord?
glad? Oh, fa-ther, ain't you glad, my Lord?

Thank God!
basso simile

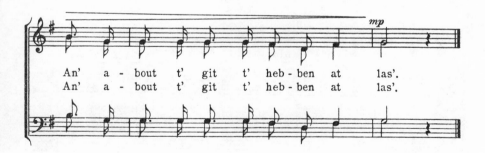

mp

An' a-bout t' git t' heb-ben at las'.
An' a-bout t' git t' heb-ben at las'.

3
Oh, sister, ain't you glad?
Sister, ain't you glad?
Oh, sister, ain't you glad, my Lord?
An' about t' git t' hebben at las'.
Refrain— I've been toilin', etc.

4
Oh, brother, ain't you glad?
Brother, ain't you glad?
Oh, brother, ain't you glad, my Lord?
An' about t' git t' hebben at las'.
Refrain— I've been toilin', etc.

Hymns of Tribulation
Keep Me From Sinkin' Down

Adagio appenato marcato portamento ♩ = 46

Hymns of Tribulation

Like a Rough and a Rolling Sea

2

The lightnings flashed,
And the thunders rolled,
Like a rough and a rolling sea.

3

The storms beat high,
And the winds blew fierce,
Like a rough and a rolling sea.

Hymns of Tribulation

Mother, Is Massa Gwine to Sell Us?

2

Gwine to sell us down in Georgia?
Yes, yes, yes!
Gwine to sell us down in Georgia?
Yes, yes, yes!
Gwine to sell us down in Georgia?
Yes, yes, yes!
O watch and pray!

3

Farewell, mother, I must lebe you.
Yes, yes, yes!
Farewell, mother, I must lebe you.
Yes, yes, yes!
Farewell, mother, I must lebe you.
Yes, yes, yes!
O watch and pray!

4

Mother, don't griebe arter me.
No, no, no!
Mother, don't griebe arter me.
No, no, no!
Mother, don't griebe arter me.
No, no, no!
O watch and pray!

5

Mother, I'll meet you in heaven.
Yes, my child!
Mother, I'll meet you in heaven.
Yes, my child!
Mother, I'll meet you in heaven.
Yes, my child!
O watch and pray!

Hymns of Tribulation

My Way's Cloudy

Oh! breth-er-en, my__ way, my way's cloud-y, my__ way, Oh, send one an-gel down, Oh! breth-er-en, my__ way, my way's cloud-y, my__ way, Oh, send one an-gel down.

Solo

mf recitando

Tutti
cresc.

Solo

1 There's fire in the east and fire in the west, Send one an-gel down, And
2 Old Sa-tan's mad and I am glad, Send one an-gel down, He
3 I'll tell you now as I told you be-fore, Send one an-gel down, To
4 This is the year of Ju-bi-lee, Send one an-gel down, The

Tutti
decresc.

D. C.

fire a-mong the Meth-o-dist, O send one an-gel down.
missed the soul he thought he had, O send one an-gel down.
the promised land I'm bound to go, O send one an-gel down.
Lord has come to set us free, O send one an-gel down.

Hymns of Tribulation

Nobody Knows de Trouble I've Seen

This song was a favorite in the Sea Islands. Once when there had been a good deal of ill feeling excited, and trouble was apprehended, owing to the uncertain action of the Government in regard to the confiscated lands on the Sea Islands, Gen. Howard was called upon to address the colored people earnestly. To prepare them to listen, he asked them to sing. Immediately an old woman on the outskirts of the meeting began "Nobody knows the trouble I've seen," and the whole audience joined in. The General was so affected by the plaintive melody, that he found it difficult to maintain his official dignity.— *Contributor*

2

One day when I was walkin' along, Oh, yes, Lord,
De element opened, an' de Love came down, Oh, yes, Lord,
I never shall forget dat day, Oh, yes, Lord,
When Jesus washed my sins away, Oh, yes, Lord,
Chorus — Oh, nobody knows de trouble I've seen, etc.

Hymns of Tribulation

No More Auction Block*

2 No more peck o' corn for me, etc.

3 No more driver's lash for me, etc.

4 No more pint o' salt for me, etc.

5 No more hundred lash for me, etc.

6 No more mistress' call for me, etc.

* Fisk Jubilee Collection, by permission

Hymns of Tribulation
Soon I Will Be Done

Molto moderato con dolemente ♩ = 60
Refrain
Tutti

Soon I will be done a-with the troub-les of the world,

Troub-les of the world, ____ The troub-les of the world,

Soon I will be done a-with the troubles of the world, Goin' home to live with God.

1 No more weeping and a-wailing, No more weeping and a-wailing,
2 I want t' meet my_ mother, I want t' meet my_ mother,
3 I want t' meet my_ Je-sus, I want t' meet my_ Je-sus,

No more weeping and a-wail-ing, I'm goin' to live with God.
I want t' meet my_ moth-er, I'm goin' to live with God.
I want t' meet my_ Je-sus, I'm goin' to live with God.

✱ Fisk Jubilee Collection, by permission

I'm So Glad Trouble Don't Last Alway

From the Collection of
R. N. D.

Refrain

Solo — I'm so glad troub-le don't last al - way, I'm so glad

troub-le don't last al - way, ___ I'm so glad troub-le don't last al -

way; O my Lord, O my Lord, what shall I do?

Solo — 1 Christ tol' the blin' man, To go to the pool and bathe,

Tutti — Christ tol' the blin' man, To go to the pool and

bathe, ___ Christ tol' the blin' man, To go to the pool and

bathe; O my Lord, O my Lord, what shall I do?

Solo — 2 Christ tol' Nic - o - de - mus, He mus' be born a - gin,

Tutti — Christ tol' Nic - o - de - mus, He mus' be born a - gin, ___

Christ tol' Nic - o - de - mus, He mus' be born a -

gin; O my Lord, O my Lord, what shall I do?

Hymns of Tribulation
I'm Troubled in Mind

The person who furnished this song, Mrs Brown of Nashville, formerly a slave, stated that she first heard it from her old father when she was a child. After he had been whipped he always went and sat upon a certain log near his cabin, and with tears streaming down his cheeks, sang this song with so much pathos that few could listen without weeping from sympathy, and even his cruel oppressors were not wholly unmoved.

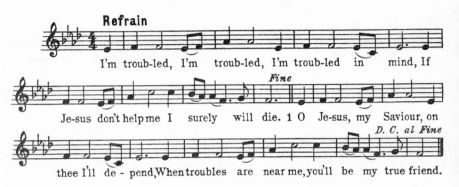

2
When ladened with trouble and burdened with grief,
To Jesus in secret I'll go for relief.
Chorus — I'm troubled, etc.

3
In dark days of bondage to Jesus I prayed,
To help me to bear it and He gave His aid.
Chorus — I'm troubled, etc.

Lord, Have Mercy

Collected by
R. N. D.

2 Save me, Jesus,
3 Save poor sinner,
4 Lord, I'm troubed, } Save me now.
5 Lord, I'm sinking,
6 When I'm dying,

APPENDIX

APPENDIX

A comparison of this edition with almost any of the previous ones will show that the way many of the Negro folk-songs are sung at present is quite different from that recorded nearly a half-century ago. In order "that nothing may be lost" the original scores of some of those that are radically different are included in the following Appendix.

Considering the vast changes in the circumstances of the Negro people in the United States since Emancipation it is remarkable that so much of the music of slavery days has remained intact. A study of differences seems to indicate that *the principle of ease* rather than mental reaction to new conditions has been the force most operative in bringing about variations from originals.

"Roll, Jordan, Roll," as given in the body of this book, is much easier to sing than the version in the Appendix; moreover the flat seventh of the earlier version is not a true tone according to our present system of music notation. It is not as low as the flat represents it to be, yet it is lower than the pitch indicated by the seventh of the scale would be without the flat. It is what Mr. Ballanta-Taylor calls a "neutral" pitch and has been for years the marvel as well as the *bête noire* of transcribers of these songs. Its occurrence in various songs has given rise to the statement often heard that Negro music cannot be properly interpreted on the piano (or any other instrument with fixed pitches).

The shifted rhythm in the chorus of "Want to Go to Heaven" and the somewhat simpler melody of "Go Tell It on the Mountain" both make for greater ease. From "Rise Up, Shepherd" a verse has fallen into disuse, while "Swing Low, Sweet Chariot" has been enriched by the muted harmonies of the chorus against the *recitative* of the leader.

It is possible that the death of Dr. Hollis Burke Frissell, for nearly twenty-five years principal of Hampton Institute, with whom the song was a great favorite, has had some effect on the rhythm of the singing of "My Lord, What a Morning!"* A chromatic note has crept into the tenor part, and very likely will remain because of its lending a touch of tender expression.

Interjectional phrases being very much the result of unconscious emotion should occasion neither surprise nor disappointment when not always found to be the same. Making an appearance for the first time in " 'Tis Me," and being sung at a higher pitch in "Couldn't Hear Nobody Pray," they point toward an increasing rather than a lessening of intensity of religious fervor in the singing of these songs with the passing of the years.

"Keep Me from Sinking Down," as it stands in the body of the book, is as it has been traditionally sung at Hampton; the foot-note to the score in the Appendix explains the reason for the other version.

For the closing piece of this volume, I have chosen a melody given me some years ago by Dr. Robert R. Moton, principal of Tuskegee Institute, while he was yet Commandant at Hampton. For several reasons its inclusion, especially as *L'Envoi*, seems appropriate: first, because of the contributor who, probably more than any other person, has had the greatest experience in conducting these songs under circumstances most conducive to bringing out the best in them; second, because of the beauty of both tune and words; and last, because it seems to best express briefly the crux of that philosophy characteristic of the Negro in his rudest estate, which in a most remarkable way sensed and voiced the transitory nature of human existence.

With an almost uncanny assurance this song addresses supernal forces; the slave speaks with a voice of command; a servant's eyes are ravished by the sight of regal joys in which by divine right he expects to share; unseen wings are summoned to do the bidding of feet broken with toil, and are never, even for a moment, expected to hesitate or fail because of the race, creed, or circumstance of him whose evocation they speed to answer. Thus are Ethiopic and Abyssinian liturgies revived on Occidental shores, and, even in the shadow of the auction block, faith is born anew.

R. Nathaniel Dett, Editor.

*Dr. Frissell often took Dr. Moton's place as "leader," singing with and directing the students in this song.

Hymns of Aspiration
Roll, Jordan, Roll*

♩ = 52

Roll, Jor-dan, roll, Roll, Jor-dan, roll, I want to go to heav-en when I die, To hear Jor-dan roll.

Fine

1 O broth - er, you ought t'have been there,
2 O sis - ter, you ought t'have been there,
3 O preach - er, you ought t'have been there,
4 O sin - ners, you ought t'have been there,

Yes, my Lord! A - sit-ting in the king-dom To hear Jor-dan roll.

D.C.

---

*This version of "Roll, Jordan, Roll" with its weird flatted seventh seems never to have been popular farther North than the Carolinas. Psychologists attribute this to a happier state of mind on the part of Negroes in the more Northern States. —Editor

Hymns of Aspiration
Want to Go to Heaven When I Die

Hymns of Christmas

Go Tell It on de Mountain

1 When I was a seek-er I sought both night an' day,
2 He made me a watchman Up-on a cit-y wall,

I ask' de Lord to help me, An' He show' me de
An' if I am a chris-tian, I am de least of

Chorus

way. Go tell it on de moun-tain,
all.

O - ver de hills an' ev - 'ry - where;

Go tell it on de moun-tain, Dat Je-sus Christ is born.

Hymns of Christmas

Rise Up, Shepherd, an' Foller

Solo

mf

1 Dere's a Star in de Eas' on Christ-mas morn,
2 If yo' take good heed to de an - gel's words,

f Chorus   Solo

Rise up, shepherd, an' fol-ler; It 'll lead t' de place where de
Rise up, shepherd, an' fol-ler; Yo'll for-get yo' flocks, yo'll for-

Chorus

Sav-iour's born, —— Rise up, shepherd, an' fol-ler;
get yo' herds, —— Rise up, shepherd, an' fol-ler;

Refrain

Leave yo' sheep and leave yo' lambs, Rise up, shepherd, an' fol-ler;

Leave yo' ewes and leave yo' rams, Rise up, shepherd, an' fol-ler;

Fol - ler, fol - ler, Rise up, shepherd, an' fol-ler;

Fol-ler de Star o' Beth-le-hem, — Rise up, shepherd, an' fol-ler.

Hymns of Death

Swing Low, Sweet Chariot

Lento con molto espressione ♩ = 50

Hymns of the Death of Christ

Were You There When They Crucified My Lord?

Adagio con molto espress. ♩ = 68

Solo

1 Were you there when they cru - ci -fied my Lord?_____
2 Were you there when they nailed Him to the tree?_____
3 Were you there when they pierced Him in the side?_____
4 Were you there when the sun re-fused to shine?_____
5 Were you there when they laid Him in the tomb?_____

(were you there?) Were you
(to the tree?) Were you
(in the side?) Were you
(were you there?) Were you
(in the tomb?) Were you

there when they cru - ci -fied my Lord? Oh!___ Sometimes it caus-es me to
there when they nailed Him to the tree? Oh!___ Sometimes it caus-es me to
there when they pierced Him in the side? Oh!___ Sometimes it caus-es me to
there when the sun re-fused to shine? Oh!___ Sometimes it caus-es me to
there when they laid Him in the tomb? Oh!___ Sometimes it caus-es me to

trem-ble, trem-ble trem-ble, Were you there when they cru - ci -fied my Lord?
trem-ble, trem-ble trem-ble, Were you there when they nailed Him to the tree?
trem-ble, trem-ble trem-ble, Were you there when they pierced Him in the side?
trem-ble, trem-ble trem-ble, Were you there when the sun re-fused to shine?
trem-ble, trem-ble trem-ble, Were you there when they laid Him in the tomb?

Hymns of Deliverance

Steal Away to Jesus

Andante assai, con molto espress. ♩ = 60

Refrain
Tutti

Steal a-way, steal a-way, Steal a-way to Je - sus.

tempo rubato poco rit.   *Fine*

Steal a-way, steal a-way home, I ain't got long to stay here.

Solo
ff con molto espressione

1 My Lord calls me, He calls me by the thun - der;
2 Green trees are bend - ing, Poor sin - ner stands a - trem - bling;
3 Tomb-stones are burst - ing, Poor sin - ner stands a - trem - bling;
4 My Lord calls me, He calls me by the light - ning;

molto morendo **Tutti**   *D. C.*

The trum-pet sounds with-in-a my soul, I ain't got long to stay here.

Hymns of Judgment

My Lord, What a Morning!

2

You'll hear de Christians shout, To wake, etc.
  Look in my God's right hand, When de stars, etc.
You'll hear de angels sing, To wake, etc.
  Look in my God's right hand, When de stars, etc.
Refrain — My Lord, what a morning, etc.

3

You'll see my Jesus come, To wake, etc.
  Look in my God's right hand, When de stars, etc.
His chariot wheels roll round, To wake, etc.
  Look in my God's right hand, When de stars, etc.
Refrain — My Lord, what a morning, etc.

Hymn of Penitence

'Tis Me

Hymns of Religious Experience

I Couldn't Hear Nobody Pray

* The interjections used here are not the only ones which can be used, but may be changed according to the emotions of the leader.

** Let this stanza be exceedingly slow, about half as fast as the others, and the Chorus very soft But go into the Refrain *a tempo*.

Hymns of Tribulation

Keep Me From Sinkin' Down

*This song was found on a fragment of a page of an old book of Negro songs. It is to be regretted that the complete book was not available in order that credit might be given to the original transcriber. The solo lines exhibit an elemental but decidedly pronounced counterpoint, based on harmonies seldom, if ever, heard now-a-days in Negro music. It is hoped that the publication by Mr. Ballanta-Taylor of the results of his research in African folksong will throw much light on the tendency of Negro music toward subdominant keys.— Editor

L'Envoi

An old Negro melody
transcribed from the singing
of Dr. Robert Russa Moton
Principal, Tuskegee Institute

Set in the form
of a chorale by
R. Nathaniel Dett

* Second verse added from a hymn by Rev. Horatius Bonar